ENCYCLOPEDIA *of* DISCOVERY

History

Conceived and produced by Weldon Owen Pty Limited
59 Victoria Street, McMahons Point, NSW, 2060, Australia
© 2001 Weldon Owen Inc.
Reprinted 2005

Chief Executive Officer: John Owen
President: Terry Newell
Publisher: Sheena Coupe
Creative Director: Sue Burk
Editorial Coordinator: Sarah Anderson
Production Manager: Louise Mitchell
Production Coordinator: Monique Layt
Vice President, International Sales: Stuart Laurence

Managing Editor: Rosemary McDonald
Project Editor: Ann B. Bingaman
Text Editors: Jane Bowring, Claire Craig
Educational Consultants: Richard L. Needham,
Deborah A. Powell
Designers: Juliet Cohen, Lyndel Donaldson, Gary Fletcher,
Kathy Gammon, Avril Makula, Kylie Mulquin, Jill Ryan
Visual Research Coordinators: Esther Beaton, Jenny Mills
Visual Researchers: Peter Barker, Karen Burgess,
Annette Crueger, Amanda Parsonage, Lorann Pendleton,
Fay Torres-Yap, Amanda Weir

Text: Judith Simpson

Illustrators: Paul Bachem; Kenn Backhaus; Andrew
Beckett/Garden Studio; Leslye Cole/Alex Lavroff &
Associates; Chris Forsey; John Crawford Fraser; Kerri
Gibbs; Mike Gorman; Ray Grinaway; Helen Halliday;
Lorraine Hannay; Adam Hook/Bernard Thornton Artists,
UK; Christa Hook/Bernard Thornton Artists, UK; Richard
Hook/Bernard Thornton Artists, UK; Keith Howland;
Janet Jones/Alex Lavroff & Associates; David Kirshner;
Mike Lamble; Robyn Latimer; Connell Lee; Avril Makula;
Shane Marsh/Linden Artists; Iain McKellar; Peter Mennim;
Paul Newman; Paul Newton; Steve Noon/Garden Studio;
Matthew Ottley; Darren Pattenden/Garden Studio; Evert
Ploeg; Tony Pyrzakowski; John Richards; Trevor Ruth;
Ray Sim; Mark Sofilas/Alex Lavroff & Associates; Sharif
Tarabay/Garden Studio; C. Winston Taylor; Steve Trevaskis;
Rod Westblade; Ann Winterbotham; David Wun

ISBN 1 74089 328 X

Color reproduction by Colourscan Co Pte Ltd
Printed by SNP Leefung Printers Ltd
Printed in China

A Weldon Owen Production

ENCYCLOPEDIA *of* DISCOVERY

History

CONSULTING EDITORS

George Hart

David Hurst Thomas

Carol Michaelson

Lorann Pendleton

Paul C. Roberts

Louise Schofield

WELDON OWEN

Contents

ANCIENT EGYPT 6

AN ANCIENT WORLD
The Black and the Red 8
Power of the Pharaohs 10
The God-kings 12
Social Order 14
People's Gods 16
Serving the Gods 18

THE WORLD BEYOND
Preparing for the Afterlife 20
Mummies in the Making 22
Journey to Osiris 24
Set in Stone 26
Great Temples 28

LIVING IN THE PAST
A River of Three Seasons 30
Working the Land 32
Family Life 34
Dressing Up 36
Writing and Education 38
Healing and Magic 40
Making Things 42
Artists at Work 44
Feasts and Festivals 46

FOREIGN AFFAIRS
Defending the Kingdom 48
Collapse of an Empire 50

ANCIENT CHINA 52

ANCIENT BEGINNINGS
The Middle Kingdom 54
The Shang Dynasty 56
The Qin Dynasty 58
The Han Dynasty 60
The Tang Dynasty 62

HEAVEN AND EARTH
Sons of Heaven 64
In Life and Death 66

LIVING IN ANCIENT CHINA
Order in Society 68
The Peasant and the Land 70
Family Life 72
Clothing and Jewelry 74
A Time to Celebrate 76
Medical Practice 78

DISCOVERY, ART AND INVENTION
Writing and Printing 80
Artists and Artisans 82
New Ideas 84

ANCIENT GREECE 86

THE GREEK WORLD
A Seafaring People 88
The Mycenaeans 90
Settling New Lands 92
City-states 94
Government and the Law 96
On Mount Olympus 98

LIVING IN ANCIENT GREECE
In the Home 100
Writing and Education 102
Dressing for the Climate 104
Making a Living 106
Meeting Place 108
Eating and Drinking 110
Festival Games 112

ARTS AND SCIENCE
Sickness and Health 114
Clay and Metal 116
Building in Stone 118

FOREIGN AFFAIRS
Going to War 120
The Macedonians 122
The Hellenistic World 124
End of an Empire 126

ANCIENT ROME   128

THE ROMAN WORLD
The Seven Hills   130
The Etruscans   132
Government   134
Worshiping the Gods   136

LIVING IN THE EMPIRE
Marriage and Home Life   138
Children and Education   140
Togas and Tunics   142
City Life   144
Country Life   146
Craft Skills   148
Staying Healthy   150
Food and Feasts   152
Spectator Sports   154

EXPANSION AND EMPIRE
Roads and Travel   156
On the March   158
Growing Empire   160
The Beginnings of Christianity   162

THE FALL OF ROME
Empire in Decline   164
The End of the Western Empire   166
Eastern Empire   168

NATIVE AMERICANS   170

THE PEOPLE
Where Did They Come From?   172
Where Did They Live?   174
What Did They Wear?   176
Life as a Child   178
Choosing a Partner   180
Games and Sport   182

ON THE MOVE
Canoes and Kayaks   184
Getting Around   186
Horses and Ponies   188

MAKING A LIVING
The Foragers   190
The Fishers   192
Making a Meal   194

HOMES
Village Life   196
Tepees   198

CEREMONIES AND RITUALS
Totems, Masks and Kachinas   200
Special Occasions   202
Ceremonial Dancing   204
Pipes and Powwows   206
Healers and Healing   208

A CHANGING WORLD
Warriors and Warfare   210
Arrival of Strangers   212
Life on a Reservation   214
Arts and Crafts   216

Glossary   218
Index   222

Ancient Egypt

- Why did ancient Egyptians wear good luck charms?

- Which god had the head of a jackal?

- Why would an ancient Egyptian mother eat a mouse?

THE CLIFFS OF THEBES
Limestone cliffs line the western
boundary of the valley at Thebes.
Pharaohs built temples on the
edge of the floodplain and tombs
in the hills beyond.

MEDITERRANEAN SEA

Alexander's Alexandria
Alexander the Great
invaded Egypt in 331 BC,
and planned a great city
called Alexandria.

Rosetta
Alexandria

LOWER EGYPT

Giza • Cairo
Memphis • • Saqqara

SINAI DESERT

Faiyum

EASTERN DESERT

The monuments of Giza
The pyramids and the sphinx at
Giza are landmarks of ancient
Egypt, visible from a great
distance across the desert.

WESTERN DESERT

• Amarna

UPPER EGYPT

Abydos •

LIBYA

Queen Hatshepsut's temple
Queen Hatshepsut, who ruled as pharaoh,
built a terraced temple at Deir el-Bahri on
the west bank of the Nile. She filled the
gardens with sweet-smelling plants.

*Valley of
the Kings*

Karnak
• Luxor
Thebes

Edfu •

Temples at Karnak
Karnak was an
important religious
center. Stone columns
with elaborately carved
tops supported the
heavy roofs of the
huge temples.

Abu Simbel
Ramesses II ordered two
huge temples to be built in
the desert at Abu Simbel
in Nubia. They were
carved out of the
sandstone cliffs.

• Abu Simbel

NUBIA

NUBIAN DESERT

CUSH

• AN ANCIENT WORLD •

The Black and the Red

People began to live beside the River
Nile many thousands of years ago.
The river cut through the desert and
provided them with water. The valley of
Upper Egypt in the south formed a long
narrow strip; the delta of Lower Egypt in
the north spread out across the river
mouth. Every year, floods washed thick mud over the
banks and left good soil behind. Early Egyptians called
this the "Black Land" and used it for growing crops.
Beyond it was the "Red Land," an immense stony waste
where it hardly ever rained and nothing useful grew.
Where the Black Land ended, the Red Land began.
A person could stand with one foot on fertile ground
and the other on dry sand. Wolves and jackals hunted
along the edges of the desert, but human enemies were
seldom able to cross it and attack ancient Egypt.

8

MARSH HUNT
The hunter felled birds with his throwing stick after his trained cat had startled them from the papyrus reeds.

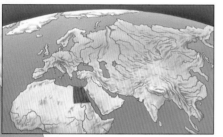

RED SEA

LAND OF THE LOTUS
People in modern times have likened ancient Egypt to a lotus plant, with its valley as the stem and its delta as the flower.

THE CIVILIZATION OF ANCIENT EGYPT

Hippopotamus hunt

New stone-age pottery

LAND OF TWO KINGDOMS
Begins about 3000 BC.
Ditches were dug to irrigate the land and villages became more established. In 3100 BC, Narmer united Upper and Lower Egypt.

Narmer's palette shows his victory

Tuthmosis IV

OLD STONE AGE
Before 12,000 BC.
The earliest Egyptians hunted lions, goats and wild cattle on land, and hippopotamuses and crocodiles in the river marshes.

NEW STONE AGE
Begins about 4500 BC.
During this period, people discovered fire for cooking. They learned to herd animals and to grow grain.

RULE OF THE PHARAOHS
2920 BC to 332 BC.
Egypt was strong for much of this time. Monuments were built and trade with foreign countries developed.

Discover more in A River of Three Seasons

Power of the Pharaohs

The civilization we call ancient Egypt started about 5,000 years ago, when the rule of the pharaohs began. They made Egypt a rich and powerful nation, admired throughout the ancient world. They also ordered the building of great temples for their gods and elaborate tombs for themselves. Some pharaohs, such as Pepy II, came to the throne when they were very young and stayed in power for many years. Sons inherited their father's throne. Pharaohs' wives were also important, but few women ever ruled the country. Teams of workers crafted beautiful objects for the pharaohs and their families. They used materials such as semi-precious stones and gold from the desert mines. The royal couple often displayed their riches in public. Processions, receptions for foreign visitors and visits to the temples were opportunities to show the power of the pharaohs.

A ROYAL JOURNEY
The magnificent royal barge gliding down the river reminded people of the wealth and importance of their god-king and his "Great Royal Wife."

THE DYNASTIES OF THE PHARAOHS

ARCHAIC PERIOD
2920 BC to 2575 BC.
Upper and Lower Egypt were united. Building programs included impressive monuments in Saqqara and Abydos.

Stone vase

OLD KINGDOM
2575 BC to 2134 BC.
This period was also known as the Age of Pyramids. Crafts and architecture developed. Picture symbols, called hieroglyphs, were used to write the texts inside the pyramids.

Female brewer

FIRST INTERMEDIATE PERIOD
2134 BC to 2040 BC.
At the end of the sixth dynasty, a series of weak pharaohs ruled. Local officials called nomarchs struggled for more power. Low Nile floods caused widespread famine.

MIDDLE KINGDOM
2040 BC to 1640 BC.
Strong pharaohs united the country again and trade revived. The twelfth-dynasty pharaohs organized canals and reservoirs for better irrigation.

King Mentuhotpe II

PEOPLE IN WAITING
Officials and tribute bearers, soldiers and slaves stood by the immense columns of the temple to welcome their pharaoh.

FIT FOR A PHARAOH
A sphinx guarded the prow. The rest of the barge was covered with gold and inlaid with semi-precious stones.

SAFE LANDING
Oarsmen were skilled at bringing the boat smoothly to rest beside the dock.

SECOND INTERMEDIATE PERIOD
1640 BC to 1550 BC.
The pharaohs lost control. The Hyksos from the Near East settled in the delta region.

NEW KINGDOM
1550 BC to 1070 BC.
Ahmose ousted the Hyksos. The pharaohs who followed him expanded Egypt's frontiers to form an empire.

Chariot

THIRD INTERMEDIATE PERIOD
1070 BC to 712 BC.
Power was divided between the pharaohs and the high priests.

LATE PERIOD
712 BC to 332 BC.
The Egyptian conquerors became the conquered. Successive invasions of Nubians, Assyrians and Persians took over Egypt. In 332 BC, Alexander the Great freed Egypt from Persian rule.

Alexander the Great

Discover more in Defending the Kingdom

11

The God-kings

An ancient Egyptian creation myth tells how the god Osiris was sent by Re, the sun-god, to rule the country. The Egyptians believed that all pharaohs were god-kings. The god-kings took part in many ceremonies. They had to dress, eat and even wash in a special way, and every day they went to the temple to offer food to their ancestors. People expected pharaohs to be physically strong, expert at hunting and able to lead the army to victory in battle. Their subjects thought the god-kings controlled the flowing and flooding of the Nile and the growth of crops, as well as the country's success in foreign trade. Everyone knelt and kissed the ground when they approached the royal person. The pharaohs continued to be worshipped even after they had died and joined the god Osiris in the kingdom of the dead.

DID YOU KNOW?

When Queen Hatshepsut's husband died, she took over government and ruled for her stepson Tuthmosis III, who was only five. She held power for about 20 years. Statues show her wearing the false beard of kingship.

MARK OF A PHARAOH
Oval shapes containing hieroglyphs were called cartouches. Two of them make up a pharaoh's name. Cartouches have helped Egyptologists decipher the ancient Egyptian language.

Haremhab

THE GREAT ROYAL WIFE

Pharaohs' wives were also regarded as gods, and shared their husbands' wealth. This painted limestone bust of Queen Nefertiti shows her wearing a crown and necklace rich with jewels. Nefertiti was the wife of Akhenaten. She helped him establish a new city at Amarna on the east bank of the River Nile in Middle Egypt. Women rarely ruled the country unless it was for a short time at the end of the dynasty when there were no men to take over. Hatshepsut was the only strong woman ruler.

COURT VISITORS
Foreigners, such as this group from the Middle East, often appeared at the pharaoh's court. They came to offer gifts or to discuss trade agreements.

White crown

Red crown

CHOICE OF CROWNS

Pharaohs might wear the white crown of Upper Egypt, the red crown of Lower Egypt, the double crown of a united Egypt, the atef crown of Osiris or the blue crown.

Double crown

Atef crown

Blue crown

COMFORT AT COURT

Slaves fanned the pharaoh and his wife on their comfortable cushioned thrones. The king held a crook and flail—symbols of power linking him to the god Osiris. He also wore a crown and a false beard.

ROYAL SEAT

Tutankhamun's wooden throne, covered in gold leaf, pictured the young king with his wife Ankhsenamon.

13

POTTERY SALE
The marketplace stalls sold many different goods.

CARRYING THE PURCHASES
Wealthy citizens had porters to carry their purchases.

• AN ANCIENT WORLD •

Social Order

Ancient Egyptian society was shaped somewhat like a pyramid. The pharaoh was at the top, then came the vizier or chief minister who organized taxation, supervised agriculture and irrigation systems, and represented the pharaoh in the law courts. There were other powerful members of government who often belonged to the royal family and nomarchs who were in charge of a region or nome. Women could own property, but they did not take part in government business. All scribes and officials were respected because they could read and write. Temple priests were also honored citizens. Craftspeople occupied a lower place in society. Peasants, who grew food and worked as laborers on the royal buildings, formed a large group at the bottom of the social pyramid. Slaves, captured in war, had no rights at all. People thought that the gods gave them their positions in society.

TO MARKET
People brought things to market to swap for what they needed.

COUNTING THE CATTLE

An ancient Egyptian's wealth was measured in cattle rather than in coins. Meketre, who was once mayor of Thebes, had a healthy herd of animals. This model from his tomb shows them being counted in front of their master and other officials. This was a yearly event of great importance. Government scribes came to record the numbers carefully on papyrus. Later, they would calculate how many beasts Meketre must give the pharaoh as a tax payment.

WOMEN'S WORK
Some tasks, such as grinding grain, baking and harvesting, spinning and weaving flax, were done more often by women than by men.

FRESH FOOD
In Egypt's hot climate, people had to shop daily for fresh provisions. Few foods were dried for storage.

WEIGHING THE GOODS
Ancient Egyptians did not use money. Stallholders weighed produce in copper weights, called debens, and priced goods accordingly. A goat worth 1 deben could be exchanged for vegetables weighing 1 deben.

People's Gods

HOME HELP
Bes had the ears, mane and tail of a lion. He brought happiness to the home and protected it from evil.

PAPYRUS PASTURE
The cow in the marsh is the goddess Hathor in disguise. She was a protector of fertility and childbirth.

Religion was a very important part of the lives of ancient Egyptians. They worshipped hundreds of gods. Some, such as the sun-god Re or Amun-Re, were honored by everyone throughout the land in a festival that lasted for a month in the flood season when farmers did no work in the fields. In addition, each of the 42 regions (nomes) adopted a different god to look after its affairs. At home, people turned to lesser gods for help with everyday problems. Many gods were depicted as animals—for example, Bastet the cat, goddess of love and joy—or as human figures with the heads of animals and birds, such as ibis-headed Thoth, god of knowledge. The gods had families too. Osiris and Isis were husband and wife with a son named Horus.

THOTH'S OTHER DISGUISE
Thoth, god of writing and knowledge, was sometimes shown as a baboon. At other times he was represented by a man with an ibis's head.

LIONESS-HEADED
The goddess Sakhmet the Powerful was shown with a woman's body and the head of a lioness.

Thoth

Re

Hathor

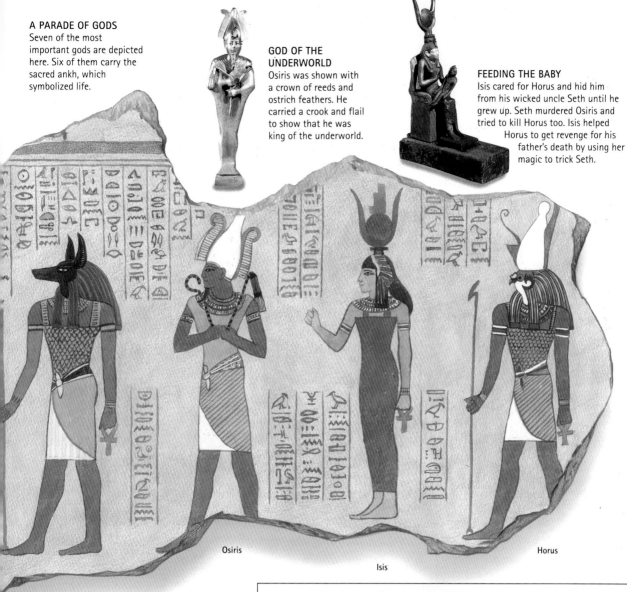

A PARADE OF GODS
Seven of the most important gods are depicted here. Six of them carry the sacred ankh, which symbolized life.

GOD OF THE UNDERWORLD
Osiris was shown with a crown of reeds and ostrich feathers. He carried a crook and flail to show that he was king of the underworld.

FEEDING THE BABY
Isis cared for Horus and hid him from his wicked uncle Seth until he grew up. Seth murdered Osiris and tried to kill Horus too. Isis helped Horus to get revenge for his father's death by using her magic to trick Seth.

Anubis

Osiris

Isis

Horus

JACKAL GOD
The god Anubis was sometimes represented as a jackal and sometimes as a man with a jackal's head. He looked after the place of mummification and supervised the priests' embalming work.

THE SUN-GOD'S DAILY JOURNEY
The ancient Egyptians traveled mainly by river boat. They believed that every 24 hours, the great sun-god Amun-Re made a voyage across the sky as though he were on the waters of the Nile. At night, he sailed through the underworld of the spirits and emerged from this dark place at sunrise each day.

Discover more in Journey to Osiris

17

Serving the Gods

FLAG BEARER
Horus, the falcon-god, sits on top of a pole that once held a flag in a temple procession.

Ancient Egyptians believed that the spirits of the gods dwelt within the temples. Many people were employed to look after these enormous buildings, which were the focus of every community. An inner sanctuary in the heart of each temple protected the statue of the god. Only the pharaoh and the high priest were allowed to enter this sacred place. The people could leave written prayers outside the temples, but they never saw the statues of the gods. Even in processions, portable shrines hid the figures from public view. Women played some part in temple ritual, but the high priests were men. They washed, dressed and applied make-up to the statues as though they were alive. The priests lived by strict rules of cleanliness. They bathed four times a day, shaved their heads and bodies and wore fine, white linen gowns.

PROVISIONS FOR A GOD
The high priest or the pharaoh carried food and drink to the sanctuary three times a day. Before each meal, they washed the statue and clothed it in fresh linen.

MUSIC FOR THE GODS
A rattle, called a sistrum, was used in temple rituals. It was the symbol of the goddess Hathor.

RITUAL OFFERING
This relief, a shallow carving in stone, shows Ramesses II offering incense to Horus.

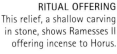

ENTERTAINING THE GODS
In the temple courtyards, women sang, danced and put on acrobatic displays for the gods.

ON FESTIVAL DAYS
The priests placed the god's statue in a shrine and carried it in procession around the outside of the temple.

SEALING THE SANCTUARY
When the high priest left the shrine, he sealed the doors with a mud seal.

TEMPLE FOR THE SUN-GOD
Treasure from successful military expeditions helped pay for the temple of Amun-Re at Karnak. Central columns, higher than a nine-storey building, are crowned with carved papyrus heads. The walls are inscribed with records of Sethos I's battle victories. The grounds once included gardens, orchards and living quarters for temple workers.

Amun-Re

FIRST SERVANT OF THE GOD
The high priests represented the pharaoh. They also supervised other priests who attended to the daily routines of the temple.

19

THE WINGS OF ISIS
One corner of Ramesses III's stone sarcophagus is carved with the protective figure of Isis with outstretched wings.

TUTANKHAMUN'S MASK
This life-size mask, engraved with magic spells, protected the head of Tutankhamun's mummy. The mask is made from gold inlaid with semi-precious stones.

• THE WORLD BEYOND •

Preparing for the Afterlife

The ancient Egyptians enjoyed life and wanted all their earthly pleasures in the afterlife. They believed that every person had vital spiritual parts. The *Ka* was the life force, created at birth and released by death; the *Ba* was like the soul. In order to live forever, the *Ka* and *Ba* had to be united with the body after death, so it was important to preserve the corpse. Poor people were buried in the desert where the sand dried their bodies. Food, tools and jewelry were laid beside them for use in the kingdom of Osiris. The wealthy could afford to have their bodies mummified and placed with their possessions in special tombs. The coffins were enclosed in large stone boxes, which were later called sarcophagi, to protect them from tomb robbers or attacks from hungry wild animals.

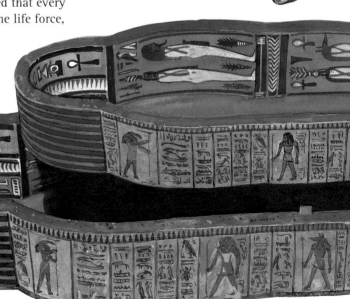

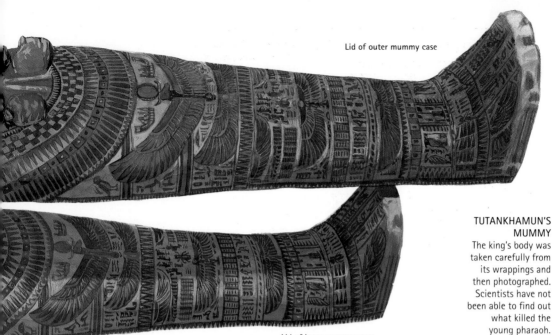

Lid of outer mummy case

Lid of inner mummy case

TUTANKHAMUN'S MUMMY
The king's body was taken carefully from its wrappings and then photographed. Scientists have not been able to find out what killed the young pharaoh.

Wrapped mummy with mask

Bottom of inner mummy case

BA BIRD
This picture of the hovering *Ba* bird is from the scribe Ani's *Book of the Dead*. It shows the spell that will return Ani's important *Ba* to his mummified body.

MUMMY CASES
Coffins made of wood or cartonnage, a kind of papier-mâché, were painted with pictures of gods, spells and many hieroglyphs praising the owner. The inner coffin fit inside one or two outer cases.

Bottom of outer mummy case

MUMMIES AND MODERN SCIENCE

Modern technology allows scientists to examine mummies without opening the coffins or damaging the bodies. At St Thomas's Hospital in London, England, the body of Tjentmutengebtiu, a 20-year-old woman, was analyzed with the help of an advanced X-ray process called CAT scanning.

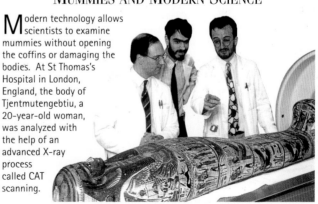

Discover more in Artists at Work

Mummies in the Making

EYES OF GOLD
In the last years of ancient Egypt, lifelike representations of eyes made from gold leaf were placed over the eye-sockets of corpses.

Mummification is the process of slowly drying a dead body to stop it from rotting. In ancient Egypt, the process took about 70 days. Embalming priests removed the liver, lungs, stomach and intestines and stored them in four special little coffins called canopic jars. Later, these were placed in the tomb beside the mummy. The priests also removed the brain, but left the heart to be weighed by the god Anubis. They washed the corpse in palm wine and covered it with a natural salt called natron to absorb the moisture. After 40 days, embalmers rubbed the skin with oils, packed the body with spices, linen, sawdust and sand to reshape it, and wrapped it in layer upon layer of linen bandages that had been soaked in resin. They placed magic spells and good luck charms between the strips. Finally, they sealed the mummy in its case.

AIR PURIFIER
The priests burned incense to sweeten the air while they prepared the mummy, working as quickly as possible.

EMBALMING WORKSHOPS
Teams of embalming priests mummified bodies in workshops where all the special tools and equipment were kept.

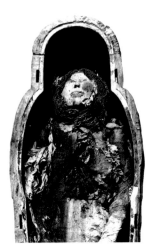

A BAD JOB
Not all embalmers were good at the job. This queen's puffed and cracked face was the result of overstuffing.

CANOPIC JARS
The Sons of Horus protected different organs: Imset for the liver, Ha'py for the lungs, Duamutef for the stomach, Qebehsenuf for the intestines.

THE FIRST MUMMY

In the beginning, Re sent Osiris and Isis to Egypt to teach the people goodness. Osiris was murdered by his jealous brother Seth, who scattered his body across the land in 14 pieces. Isis collected the parts and magically bound them together with cloth strips, making the first Egyptian mummy. Isis then became a bird, enfolded Osiris in her wings and brought him to life.

STANDING IN FOR ANUBIS

The priest in charge wore a jackal mask that symbolized Anubis, the god of the dead and mummification.

LUCKY CHARMS

Charms, called amulets, were supposed to bring luck in the afterlife. The embalmers folded them into the wrapping strips.

TREASURE OF THE TOMB

Tutankhamun's tomb contained fine gold jewelry. He wore this falcon on his chest.

THE ART OF EMBALMING

The hot, dry air of Egypt helped to preserve bodies, but the embalmers' skills were also very important. Mummies from the New Kingdom period show the best methods of preserving and wrapping.

Discover more in Healing and Magic

23

Journey to Osiris

BOOK OF THE DEAD
Sheets of papyrus covered with magic spells for the afterlife were placed in people's tombs.

The "Opening of the Mouth" was one of the most important funeral ceremonies in the final preparation of the mummy. The deceased's family recited spells while priests sprinkled water and used special instruments to touch the mummy on the lips. Without this ritual, they believed, the dead person would not be able to eat, drink or move around in the afterlife. Before anyone could qualify for eternal life, the stern judge Anubis weighed their heart against the Feather of Truth to see how well they had behaved on Earth. Anubis threw the unworthy hearts to the monster Ammit, "Devourer of the Dead," and the owners went no further. Those who passed the test continued on the dangerous and difficult journey to the kingdom of Osiris. Magic symbols painted on the mummy's case were designed to protect the traveler along the way.

WORKERS FOR ETERNITY
Nobody wanted to work in the afterlife. Model servants called shabtis were placed in the tombs to obey the god Osiris's commands.

| Hunefer | Anubis | Anubis | Ammit, Devourer of the Dead | Thoth |

ESSENTIALS FOR THE AFTERLIFE

We know much about the lives of ancient Egyptians from the contents of their tombs. Tutankhamun's tomb contained his childhood toys, 116 baskets of fruit, 40 jars of wine and boxes of roast duck, bread and cake. Musicians were buried with their instruments and women with their beauty kits. Eye make-up was included for everyone. Model boats provided transportation to the kingdom of Osiris.

STRANGE BUT TRUE

Thousands of mummified cats were found in many tombs. In the nineteenth century, about 300,000 cat mummies were shipped to England where they were ground up into garden fertilizer.

MUMMIFIED MENAGERIE

People thought that animals were messengers of the gods, and many were mummified, including calves, crocodiles and cats.

WEIGHING THE HEART

This is the mummy's most challenging moment. Ammit sits beneath the scales, hungry for sinful hearts. The scribe god, Thoth, takes notes. If all goes well, Osiris will welcome the newcomer, Hunefer.

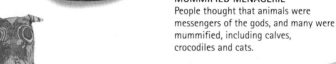

Hunefer   Horus   Osiris

Set in Stone

Many ancient Egyptian stone monuments still stand in the desert today. Although moisture, wind, sandstorms and tourists have damaged them, the pyramids, tombs, temples and colossal statues tell us much about the ideas, beliefs and technology of the people who built them. These incredibly complicated projects required expert skills and a huge workforce. Astronomers studied the stars to determine the best sites, mathematicians and architects calculated the measurements, stonemasons shaped the blocks, and overseers organized the teams of several thousand laborers. Craftsmen worked soft stones with bronze and copper chisels. They pounded harder rocks with balls of dolerite, then rubbed the surface smooth with quartz sand. The Great Pyramids at Giza were faced originally with gleaming white Tura limestone and may have been capped with gold.

SHIPPING THE STONE
Carpenters built cargo vessels at the Nile shipyards to carry stone blocks from the quarries to the building sites.

THE PYRAMIDS OF GIZA
Khufu's Great Pyramid, the biggest of three massive pyramids at Giza, is the largest stone building in the world. It is 479 ft (146 m) high and contains nearly two-and-a-half million blocks of limestone.

26

FALSE DOOR
Tombs had false doors decorated with prayers and the owners' names. They were sacred places for the living to leave offerings for the dead.

THE PYRAMIDS AND THE STARS

We know from hieroglyphs on the pyramid walls that the ancient Egyptians likened their gods to the stars. Some scientists think that the arrangement of the three Great Pyramids on Earth matches Orion's belt in the sky. The buildings are placed in a line with the smaller one slightly to the left, just as the three stars in the constellation are aligned.

Orion

THE GIZA SPHINX
This huge sphinx, cut from rock, guarded the pyramids at Giza. The statue had a human head (representing intelligence) on a lion's body (a sign of strength). Together they symbolized royal power.

DID YOU KNOW?

Building measurements on the pyramids are very precise. The stone slabs on the outside of the Great Pyramid fit so snugly side by side that a hair cannot be pushed into the joints between them.

FAMILY AFFECTION
A painted limestone statue of the priest Meresankh and his two daughters was found in his tomb.

Hatshepsut ordered her great temple to be built on the west bank of the Nile. Sloping ramps connected terraces that jutted out from the rocky backdrop on three levels. By the end of the nineteenth century, little remained except a pile of rubble and sand.

COLORED COLUMNS

The temple of the goddess Isis stands on the island of Philae. When this lithograph was made in 1846, some color still remained on the columns in the hall.

• THE WORLD BEYOND •

Great Temples

Many pharaohs ordered temples to be constructed for themselves as well as for the gods. Some of the temples were attached to pharaohs' tombs, erected in separate places or added to other buildings such as the one at Karnak. Temple complexes included huge statues, soaring columns, school rooms, storehouses and workshops, and spacious gardens. By the time Ramesses II came to power in 1290 BC, many magnificent monuments had already been built throughout ancient Egypt. He added several others during his reign of more than 60 years. The most impressive one was at Abu Simbel in the Nubian desert. The laborers chipped away the side of a hill to make the south front and then hollowed out a vast space behind it for the interior. Hatshepsut, Amenophis III, Sethos I and Ramesses III were also great temple builders.

ON A GRAND SCALE

Massive granite statues of Ramesses II stood inside and outside his temple at Abu Simbel. A single foot was taller than an adult. Shallow reliefs, carved on the north and south walls, record Ramesses II's battle victories.

THE COLOSSI OF MEMNON

Two colossal stone statues are all that remain of Amenophis III's monument on the Nile's west bank.

DID YOU KNOW?

Twice a year, the shadowy interior of Ramesses II's temple is pierced by the rays of the rising sun, which illuminate the four statues in the temple's sanctuary.

RESCUING ABU SIMBEL

When the Aswan Dam was built across the River Nile in the 1960s, it created Lake Nasser. Many of the Nubian temples were moved to prevent them from being flooded.

A River of Three Seasons

TRAVELING SOUTH
The hieroglyph "to travel south" was a boat in full sail catching the northerly wind to help propel the craft upstream.

TRAVELING NORTH
River transport and walking were the main means of traveling. The hieroglyph "to travel north" was a boat with the sail down.

When the Greek traveler Herodotus saw ancient Egypt he called it "the gift of the Nile," and nobody has ever described it better. The river was a highway for transport and trade. It provided fish and larger game in the form of hippopotamuses and crocodiles. It sustained marshes where papyrus reeds and lotus plants grew and where waterfowl could be caught for food. It supplied water for drinking and washing. Every year, almost without fail, floodwaters from the lakes and mountain springs of eastern Africa, which fed the Nile's tributaries, washed down fertile silt. The river divided the farmers' calendar into three seasons. The flood time, the "time of inundation" when all work stopped, lasted from July to October. The "time of emergence," allotted to plowing and sowing, ran from November to February. Finally, the "time of harvest" occupied March to June.

DID YOU KNOW?

It was more usual for men to wash dirty laundry in the river. Women were excused from these duties because of the constant threat from dangerous crocodiles along the river banks.

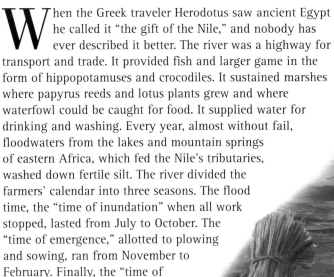

FISHING ON THE NILE
Fish from the river could be harpooned, caught with hooks and lines, or swept up in nets made from papyrus twine. They were part of the diet of ancient Egyptians.

PAPYRUS FOR MANY PURPOSES

Many years ago, papyrus grew plentifully along the banks of the Nile and in the delta swamps. The ancient Egyptians used it to make excellent paper. Some river boats were crafted from bundles of papyrus stalks; others were rigged with strong ropes made from its twisted fibers. This reed could also be woven into boxes, baskets, mats, sieves and sandals.

HUNTING GEESE
This scene from a tomb shows the sport of wealthy Egyptians—hunting with throwsticks.

SPEAR FISHING
This statuette shows Tutankhamun about to hurl his spear, probably into a hippopotamus. In his left hand he holds a cord for binding his prey.

Working the Land

The ancient Egyptians depended on the yearly cycle of flooding, sowing, and harvesting. Low floods and insufficient soil for the crops meant famine. During the growing season, a network of canals and ditches carried water to the fields. Farmers cultivated barley, emmer wheat, vegetables and fruit. Flax was another important crop. Birds and insects often invaded the fields, and sometimes violent wind storms flattened the ripening grain. Reapers, who were always men, harvested beneath the hot sun. They listened to flute music and prayed to Isis as they worked. Women never handled tools with blades. They winnowed grain, tossing it into the air so that the wind blew away the light stalks and the heavier seeds fell to the ground. Women also helped to make wine and beer and pressed oil from nuts and plants. Besides crops, farmers raised cattle, sheep, goats, ducks and geese for food. Tax assessors came every year to gauge the amount of produce that was owed to the government.

WHAT DOES THE GARDEN GROW?
The trees with the small fruit are date palms. The ancient Egyptians used dates to sweeten food.

THE FARMING SCHEDULE
Farmers worked by the rise and fall of the Nile in a yearly cycle. They never needed fertilizers because the flood soil was so rich.

HARVESTING
At harvest time, every healthy villager worked in the fields. Men cut the crop with sickles. Women and children bound the stalks into sheaves and separated the grain from the chaff.

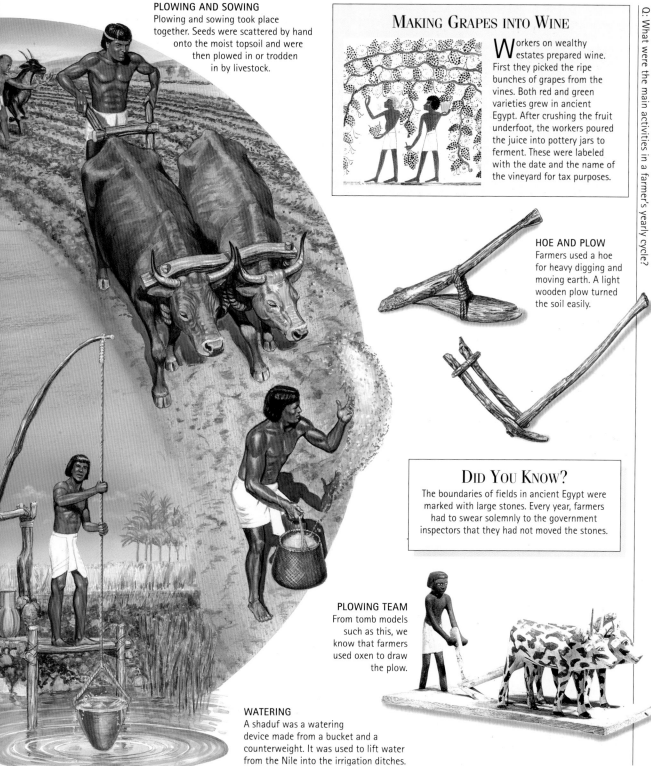

PLOWING AND SOWING

Plowing and sowing took place together. Seeds were scattered by hand onto the moist topsoil and were then plowed in or trodden in by livestock.

MAKING GRAPES INTO WINE

Workers on wealthy estates prepared wine. First they picked the ripe bunches of grapes from the vines. Both red and green varieties grew in ancient Egypt. After crushing the fruit underfoot, the workers poured the juice into pottery jars to ferment. These were labeled with the date and the name of the vineyard for tax purposes.

HOE AND PLOW

Farmers used a hoe for heavy digging and moving earth. A light wooden plow turned the soil easily.

DID YOU KNOW?

The boundaries of fields in ancient Egypt were marked with large stones. Every year, farmers had to swear solemnly to the government inspectors that they had not moved the stones.

PLOWING TEAM

From tomb models such as this, we know that farmers used oxen to draw the plow.

WATERING

A shaduf was a watering device made from a bucket and a counterweight. It was used to lift water from the Nile into the irrigation ditches.

33

IN SERVICE
Servants worked on wealthy estates. They did housework and tended the gardens, crops and livestock.

FAMILY CELEBRATION
This tomb painting is like a family photograph. It shows Inhirkha with his wife, son and grandchildren.

AT HOME
The home was a place in which the family could relax. Bigger houses had spacious living quarters with painted walls and high windows, without glass, to help keep the air cool. All homes had places for statues of the household gods.

• LIVING IN THE PAST •

Family Life

Most people in ancient Egypt lived in villages of sun-baked brick houses crammed close together. These had square rooms with small windows and flat roofs that were often used for cooking. The rich, who were able to employ servants, lived in grander homes with gardens. Twice a day, women fetched water and filled the huge clay vessels that stood in the courtyard or by the doorway of every house. People had very little furniture, especially in the poorer homes. Stools, beds and small tables were the most common pieces; chairs were a sign of importance. Ancient Egyptians usually married within their own social group. Girls became brides when they were about 12; boys married at about 14.

TIME FOR BED
Beds were made from wood and woven reeds, and had wooden head-rests for pillows. People did not use bed sheets.

STRANGE BUT TRUE
Animals were part of the household. When a pet cat died, the whole family shaved off their eyebrows as a sign of mourning.

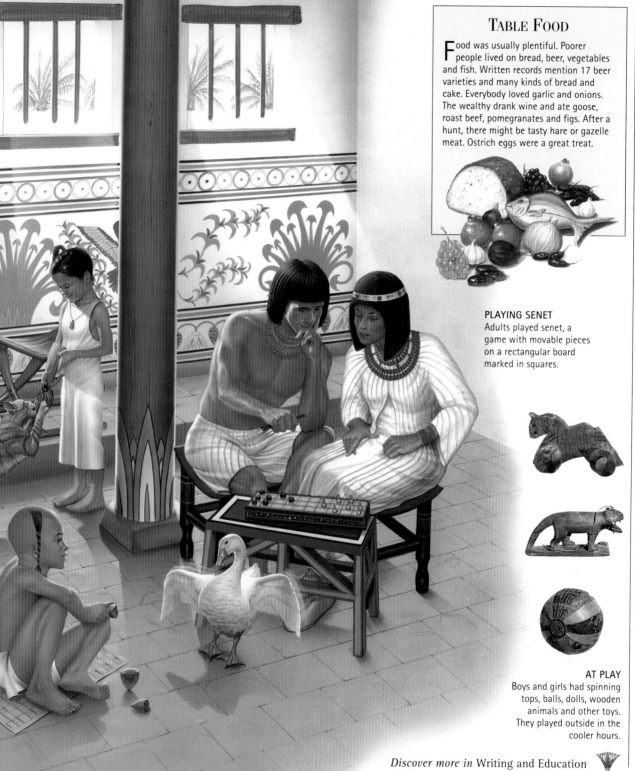

TABLE FOOD

Food was usually plentiful. Poorer people lived on bread, beer, vegetables and fish. Written records mention 17 beer varieties and many kinds of bread and cake. Everybody loved garlic and onions. The wealthy drank wine and ate goose, roast beef, pomegranates and figs. After a hunt, there might be tasty hare or gazelle meat. Ostrich eggs were a great treat.

PLAYING SENET
Adults played senet, a game with movable pieces on a rectangular board marked in squares.

AT PLAY
Boys and girls had spinning tops, balls, dolls, wooden animals and other toys. They played outside in the cooler hours.

Discover more in Writing and Education

35

Dressing Up

ROYAL SANDALS
The upper soles of Tutankhamun's sandals showed Egypt's enemies. He crushed them as he walked.

People in ancient Egypt dressed in light linen clothing made from flax. Weavers used young plants to produce fine, almost see-through fabric for the wealthy, but most people wore garments of coarser texture. The cloth was nearly always white. Pleats, held in place with stiffening starch, were the main form of decoration, but sometimes a pattern of loose threads was woven into the cloth. Slaves or servants, who came from foreign lands, had dresses of patterned fabric. Men dressed in loincloths, kilts and tunic-style shirts. Women had simple, ankle-length sheath dresses with a shawl or cloak for cooler weather. Children usually wore nothing at all. Men and women, rich and poor, owned jewelry and used make-up, especially eye paint. Everybody loved perfume and rubbed scented oils into their skin to protect it against the harsh desert winds.

EYE COLOR
Favorite eye shadows were green powdered malachite and black crushed lead ore.

REFLECTIONS
Polished bronze or copper mirrors were valued possessions. Their roundness and brightness suggested the sun's life-giving power. Poorer people checked their reflections in water.

THE MEANING OF SPOTS
Some priests wore leopard skins over their shoulders to show their importance. Here, Princess–priestess Nefertiabt is wearing a black-spotted panther skin.

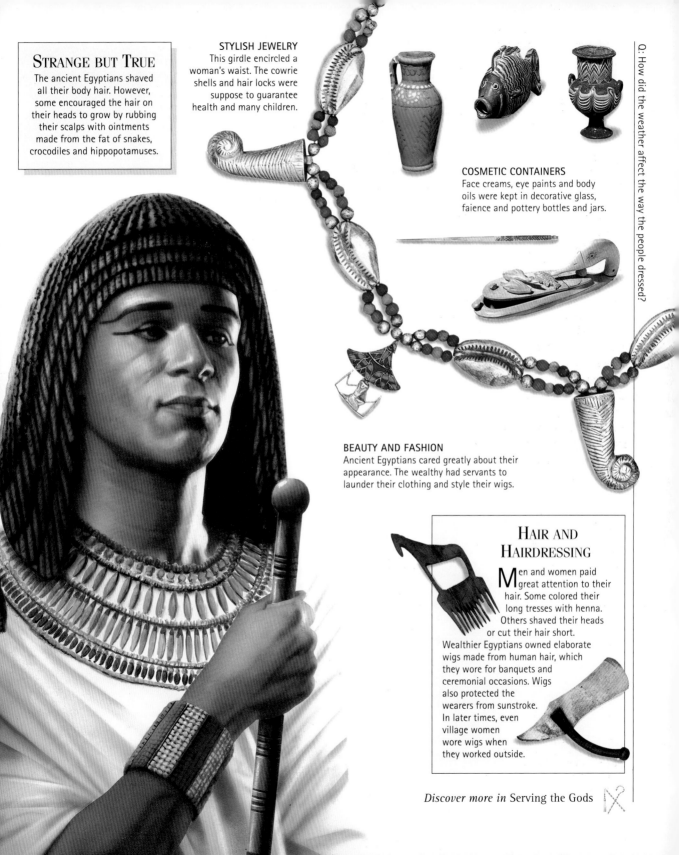

STRANGE BUT TRUE

The ancient Egyptians shaved all their body hair. However, some encouraged the hair on their heads to grow by rubbing their scalps with ointments made from the fat of snakes, crocodiles and hippopotamuses.

STYLISH JEWELRY

This girdle encircled a woman's waist. The cowrie shells and hair locks were suppose to guarantee health and many children.

COSMETIC CONTAINERS

Face creams, eye paints and body oils were kept in decorative glass, faience and pottery bottles and jars.

BEAUTY AND FASHION

Ancient Egyptians cared greatly about their appearance. The wealthy had servants to launder their clothing and style their wigs.

HAIR AND HAIRDRESSING

Men and women paid great attention to their hair. Some colored their long tresses with henna. Others shaved their heads or cut their hair short. Wealthier Egyptians owned elaborate wigs made from human hair, which they wore for banquets and ceremonial occasions. Wigs also protected the wearers from sunstroke. In later times, even village women wore wigs when they worked outside.

Discover more in Serving the Gods

Writing and Education

Ancient Egyptians used picture writing, called hieroglyphs, for inscriptions in the tombs and temples. Scribes would tell their sons that to be a scribe "is greater than any other profession." Student scribes took up to ten years to memorize the several hundred hieroglyphic signs. They also had lessons in astronomy, mathematics, astrology, practical arts and games and sports. Classroom discipline was strict and teachers believed that "the ears of a boy are on the back. He listens only when he is beaten." The boys who did not become scribes followed in their fathers' footsteps, becoming perhaps farmers or carpenters. Girls stayed at home and learned music, dancing and housekeeping skills from their mothers.

TAKING NOTE
Students learned hieratic script first. This running writing was much quicker to do than hieroglyphs.

PRACTICE MAKES PERFECT
Students practiced writing on broken bits of stone called ostraca.

HIERATIC SCRIPT
Scribes learned hieratic writing for listing taxes and recording accounts, and hieroglyphs for writing on tomb walls and monuments.

DID YOU KNOW?

Egypt officially converted to Christianity when the Roman Empire took over in AD 324. Egyptian writing was banned because the Romans considered it to be pagan. People forgot how to write hieroglyphs and nobody learned how to read them. As a result, hieroglyphs became a lost language.

Owl

Water

Bread

EVERLASTING WRITING

Carved in hard granite, this cross-legged scribe will write forever on the papyrus spread between his knees.

PAPER FROM REEDS

Paper was made from thinly sliced papyrus stems. One layer was placed on another and the plant's juices glued them together.

Man

Arm

Reed

READING THE STONE

Inscriptions on the Rosetta Stone were the key to reading the pyramid texts and other ancient Egyptian writing. The top band is in hieroglyphs. The middle band is in demotic script, a later form of hieratic writing. The bottom band is in Greek. The stone was discovered in 1799. By 1822, Jean-François Champollion, a French scholar, had deciphered some of the letters.

Mouth

WRITING KIT

A scribe's tools consisted of a palette of colored paints and brushes made from reeds.

Flax

Basket

SCRIBE SCHOOL

The boys learned to read and write in groups by copying and reciting texts with wise messages that taught them how to behave properly.

Discover more in Social Order

TAWERET
Taweret protected pregnant women. She was depicted as part hippopotamus and part woman, with the legs of a lion.

CROOKED BACK
Some statues and paintings show bone deformities. This hunchback may have had tuberculosis of the spine.

SWEET DREAMS
This hippopotamus ivory wand was used to protect a sleeper from attacks by poisonous night creatures.

EYE OF HORUS
As the two gods struggled for power, Seth tore out Horus's eye. It was magically restored and became a symbol of protective watchfulness.

• LIVING IN THE PAST •

Healing and Magic

Doctors in ancient Egypt set broken bones with wooden splints bound with plant fibers, dressed wounds with oil and honey, and performed surgery with knives, forceps and metal or wooden probes. They had cures for many diseases, some of which they thought were caused by worms, such as the "hefet" worm in the stomach or the "fenet" worm that gnawed teeth. Physicians knew that the heart "spoke" through the pulse, but they also thought it controlled everything that happened in the body and all thoughts and feelings. They did not realize that the brain was important. Plant remedies were popular. Garlic was prescribed for snakebite, to gargle for sore throats and to soothe bruises. Doctors used a vulture's quill to apply eyedrops containing celery juice. When practical medicine failed, physicians turned to magic. People wore amulets to ward off accident and sickness. They also thought some of the gods had healing powers.

A CRIPPLING DISEASE
Priest Remi's shorter, thinner leg was probably the result of polio. He would have had this illness as a child.

GOOD LUCK CHARMS

People in ancient Egypt believed that amulets protected them from harm. They wore them as personal jewelry and were buried with them for use in the afterlife. The fish amulet on the girl's braid guarded her against water accidents, such as drowning or being taken by crocodiles. The Bes amulet around her neck saved her from household dangers.

MOTHER AND CHILD

This wooden amulet shows a mother with her baby. It was supposed to ensure a safe childbirth.

WHAT MUMMIES CAN TELL US

Seqenenre II's preserved head shows the severe wounds from which he died. Through autopsies and X-ray examinations of mummies, experts have found out much about the health problems of the ancient Egyptians. They suffered from many of the sicknesses we do, but had no immunization against infectious diseases such as smallpox and polio. Some mummies have badly decayed teeth. Grit and sand in their bread may have worn away their teeth's outer surface, or perhaps ancient Egyptians ate too many cakes sweetened with honey and dates.

Making Things

Many of the objects that tell us how people lived in ancient Egypt were made by potters, stonemasons, carpenters, glassmakers, leatherworkers, metalworkers and jewelers. Most of the cloth made by spinners and weavers has perished, but we know much about their work from friezes in the tombs. The pharaohs kept whole villages of highly skilled craftspeople employed on building projects. Stone for temples, pyramids and statues was collected from the surrounding desert, and copper and gold were plentiful. Some materials had to be imported, particularly timber, ivory and semi-precious stones such as lapis lazuli and turquoise. As the ancient Egyptians did not use money, workers received their wages in clothes, lodging, bread, onions and beer. Craftspeople worked in communal workshops. Everything they did was part of a team effort and they did not receive special praise for their individual skills.

ISSUING MATERIALS
Metals were weighed before work began. The scales had pans on each end of a horizontal beam resting on a vertical support.

Ax

Saw

EAR ORNAMENTS
Men and women wore earrings and ear studs. They were sometimes made from a glass-like material called faience.

WORKING WITH WOOD
Woodworkers built or carved furniture. Some of their tools, such as saws and chisels, have not changed much through the years.

Adze

PRODUCTION LINE
This crowded workshop shows goldsmiths, carpenters, jewelers and engravers at work.

FIRE HAZARDS
Working with the hot fire day after day damaged the smelters' lungs and eyes. They were often burned by flying cinders.

STRANGE BUT TRUE

The first recorded strike in history took place near Thebes, where builders had waited two months for their wages. They refused to work and chanted "we are hungry" until they were paid.

FAIENCE BOWL

This bowl is patterned with fish swimming between lotus buds. The lotus, which opens at sunrise and closes at sunset, symbolizes rebirth.

BURNING BRIGHT

Smelters had to heat the metal ore in a container to burn off the impurities before they could use the molten metal. They made the fire burn fiercely by blowing on it through hollow reeds tipped with clay nozzles.

WOMEN AT WORK

Women did most of the weaving in ancient Egypt. This wooden model from chancellor Meketre's tomb shows the activity in the textile workshop on his estate. Some workers are walking around spinning linen thread from flax fibers. This will be woven into cloth. The weavers squatting down are operating the two horizontal looms on the floor.

BURIED TREASURE

This solid gold vase was found near the temple of ancient Bubastis. It is hammered in a corn-cob pattern.

BLOWN GLASS

Glassmakers did not learn the blowing technique until the Roman period. Before that, molten glass was molded around a core.

Discover more in The God-kings

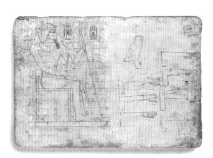

PERFECTING THE ART
This board shows a practice drawing of Tuthmosis III within a grid. The artist seemed to have trouble with the arm hieroglyph.

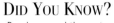

HEADS RIGHT, EYES FRONT
Artists drew people's eyes and shoulders as if they were seeing them from the front. All other parts of the body were drawn sideways. The left leg was always shown in front of the right.

PAINTING SEQUENCE
First, a stonemason smoothed the wall and covered it with a layer of thin plaster. This surface was marked with a square grid made by string dipped in red paint.

• LIVING IN THE PAST •

Artists at Work

Ancient Egyptian paintings told stories about people's lives and what they expected to happen to them after they died and met their gods. Artists painted detailed scenes on houses, temple pillars and the vast walls of tombs, where well-organized teams worked by lamplight in difficult and stuffy conditions. They followed carefully prepared plans of what to paint and strict rules about the way to show figures and objects. The outline scribes always drew important people larger than anyone else who appeared in the picture. Painters used pigments made from crushed rocks and minerals—green from powdered malachite, red from iron oxide—which they mixed with egg white and gum arabic. The colors in many of the tombs and temples are still as fresh and brilliant as when they were first brushed on the walls more than 5,000 years ago.

PAPYRUS PAINTING
The spells and texts for a person's *Book of the Dead* were painted in bright colors on sheets of papyrus.

GRACEFUL WOMAN
Paint was applied to the plaster-coated cloth that covered the wood on this coffin lid.

44

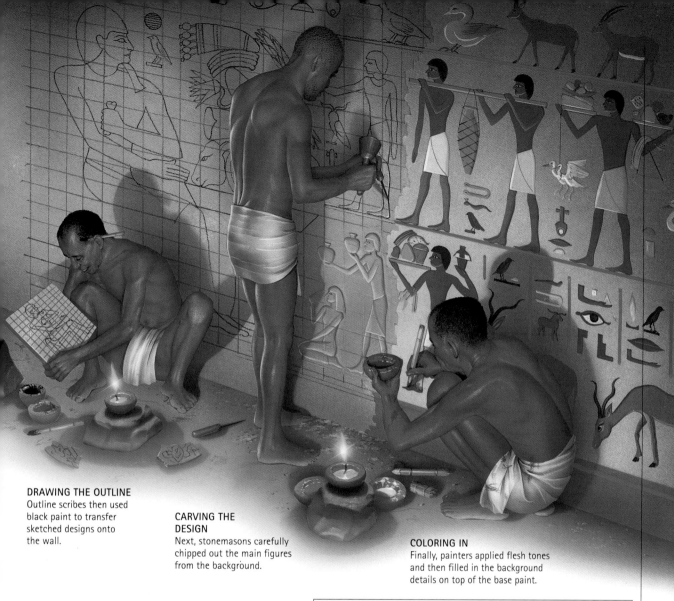

DRAWING THE OUTLINE
Outline scribes then used black paint to transfer sketched designs onto the wall.

CARVING THE DESIGN
Next, stonemasons carefully chipped out the main figures from the background.

COLORING IN
Finally, painters applied flesh tones and then filled in the background details on top of the base paint.

PAINTING EQUIPMENT
Artists' tools included palettes for diluting paint and wooden brushes with split ends for painting.

AKHENATEN'S STYLE

Pharaoh Akhenaten introduced some changes to the style of art during his 17-year rule. In his city at Amarna, dedicated to the sun-god he called Aten, the artists and sculptors used a more lifelike way of portraying people. This scene, carved in relief, shows Akhenaten giving an earring to his daughter. Queen Nefertiti holds two younger daughters.

KEEPING THE BEAT
These broken pieces of clappers, made of ivory, were once part of percussion instruments musicians used to beat out dance rhythms.

GRACEFUL GYMNASTICS
Dancers performed somersaults, back bends and high-kicks. Weighted discs on the ends of their pigtails swung with the rhythmic movement.

• LIVING IN THE PAST •

Feasts and Festivals

One hieroglyphic inscription says "be joyful and make merry." Wealthy people loved to invite friends to their homes to share great feasts. The food was plentiful and the wine flowed freely. The hosts hired storytellers, dancers and other entertainers. Ancient Egyptian musicians played many instruments including flutes, clarinets, oboes, lutes, harps, tambourines, cymbals and drums. Poorer people enjoyed themselves on holidays for royal occasions, such as the crowning of a pharaoh, and at yearly harvest and religious festivals. Huge crowds gathered for a "coming forth" when the statue of a god was carried in procession outside the temple. Music and acrobatic displays were part of these parades. People made bouquets, garlands and collars from fresh flowers for private banquets and public festivals.

PERFUMED AIR
Scented cones on the hair melted slowly during a banquet. The perfumed grease released a pleasant fragrance as it ran down over wigs and clothes.

TABLE MANNERS
Banquet guests sat around low tables. They ate with their fingers and afterwards servants brought water to wash their hands.

WELCOME GUESTS
Servants handed out scented hair cones at the door. Children often joined in the festivities.

FESTIVAL OF OPET

The Opet Festival, a yearly holiday, took place during the Nile flood. By the time Ramesses III reigned in 1194 BC, it lasted for 27 days. The statue of the great sun-god Amun-Re, attended by the pharaoh and priests, was carried in procession from Karnak temple south to Luxor temple, as shown above. After special ceremonies, the statue was returned to Karnak.

DID YOU KNOW?

Men and women never danced together in ancient Egypt. Dance routines included graceful acrobatics and gymnastics.

THE CAT GODDESS
Bastet, the cat goddess, was the daughter of Re. Her yearly festival was celebrated throughout the land.

AMUSING THE GUESTS
Storytelling and poetry recitals often began the feast. The entertainment became noisier and more energetic as the feasting progressed.

Discover more in Serving the Gods

47

Defending the Kingdom

CLOSE COMBAT
Daggers and short swords were deadly weapons for hand-to-hand fighting at close range. The blades were riveted to the handles.

For centuries, ancient Egyptians needed no permanent army. Egyptians seldom had to defend themselves against enemies, other than Libyan tribes who attacked occasionally from the Western Desert. After the Middle Kingdom, however, the Hyksos from the Near East seized Lower Egypt. They had curved swords, strong bows, body armor and horse-drawn chariots. The Egyptians copied these weapons and began training efficient soldiers. Their new army drove out the hated Hyksos and pushed them back through Palestine and Syria. Prisoners of war were forced to join the army or work as slaves. Egyptians built mudbrick forts, with massive towers surrounded by ditches, to defend their borders. Later, Ramesses III formed a navy of wooden galleys powered by oars and sails and trapped the slower sailing ships of pirates invading from the Mediterranean Sea.

TUTANKHAMUN'S CHARIOT
This scene shows a victorious Tutankhamun alone in his chariot. In real life he would have had a driver with him.

PRISONERS OF WAR
Enemies of the pharaoh were always shown with their hands bound or handcuffed.

DID YOU KNOW?
Lions represented courage in ancient Egypt. One poem said that Ramesses II fought "like a fierce lion in a valley of goats."

CEREMONIAL AX
This ceremonial ax belonged to the pharaoh Ahmose. The blade shows scenes celebrating his success in driving the Hyksos out of Egypt.

THE RULES OF WAR
A king in the ancient world led his army to fight the enemy on an open battlefield. The army waited for a signal to begin. There were few surprise attacks and no battles after dark.

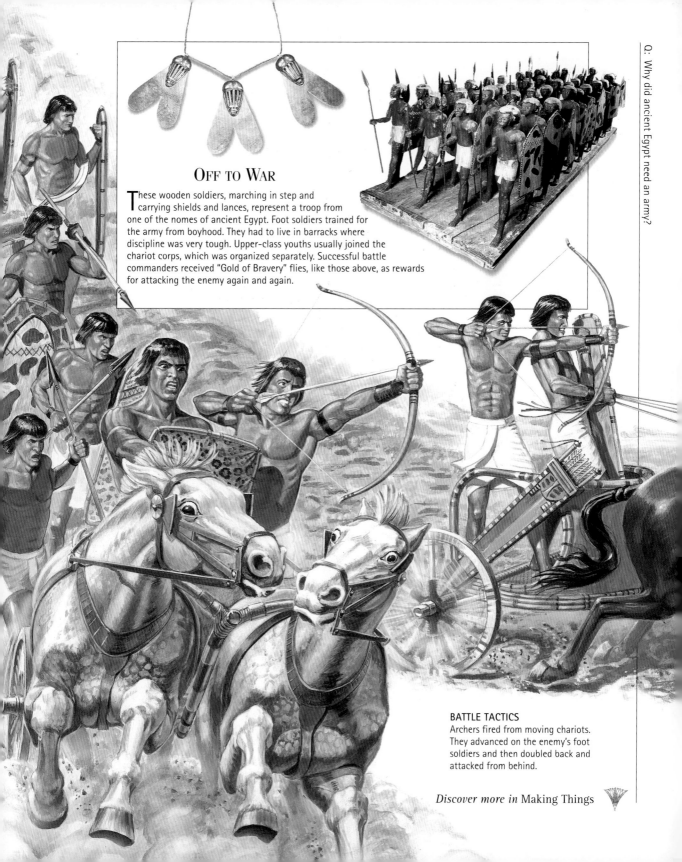

OFF TO WAR

These wooden soldiers, marching in step and carrying shields and lances, represent a troop from one of the nomes of ancient Egypt. Foot soldiers trained for the army from boyhood. They had to live in barracks where discipline was very tough. Upper-class youths usually joined the chariot corps, which was organized separately. Successful battle commanders received "Gold of Bravery" flies, like those above, as rewards for attacking the enemy again and again.

BATTLE TACTICS

Archers fired from moving chariots. They advanced on the enemy's foot soldiers and then doubled back and attacked from behind.

Discover more in Making Things

MIXED RELIGION
Although Greek pharaohs worshipped their own gods, relief carvings on the temple of Edfu show Ptolemy III and Ptolemy XII with Egyptian deities.

DRINKING CUPS
This Nubian pottery was made on a wheel and decorated with painted and stamped designs.

CHANGING GOVERNMENT
After the Nubian invasion, ancient Egypt was overrun repeatedly by foreigners. For more than a thousand years, power in the ancient world shifted from one conqueror to another.

PERSIANS IN POWER
The Persians introduced camels into ancient Egypt. These could move across the desert from one oasis to another.

• FOREIGN AFFAIRS •

Collapse of an Empire

Many of the pharaohs who came after Ramesses III were not strong rulers. Their subjects began to disobey the laws, and robbers plundered the tombs. Meanwhile, other countries in the ancient world were growing stronger. Foreign conquerors overran the Egyptian empire and invaded the country itself—first the Nubians, then the Assyrians and later the Persians. Alexander the Great brought his army to help the Egyptians expel the Persians. Ptolemy, one of Alexander's generals, founded a dynasty whose rulers spoke Greek and worshipped Greek gods. The Romans took over from the Greeks. Christianity spread through the Roman Empire and came to ancient Egypt. When the Arabs invaded in the seventh century AD, Fustat became their first capital, Islam became the state religion and Arabic became the official language.

GOLD COIN
The Greeks brought coins into Egypt. Pharaoh Ptolemy I is portrayed on this gold piece.

50

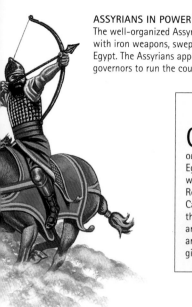

ASSYRIANS IN POWER
The well-organized Assyrian army, equipped with iron weapons, swept through ancient Egypt. The Assyrians appointed Egyptian governors to run the country.

CLEOPATRA
Cleopatra VII was the last Greek pharaoh and the only one who learned the Egyptian language. She was supported by two Roman generals, Julius Caesar and Mark Antony. When Augustus gained power over the Roman Empire, he declared war on Antony and Cleopatra and defeated them in 31 BC. Augustus arrived in Alexandria and demanded Cleopatra's surrender. She was too proud to give in and committed suicide.

ROMANS IN POWER
Emperor Augustus gained power in 30 BC. The Romans sent gold from the desert mines back to Rome.

ROMAN PORTRAIT
Portraits on coffins became more lifelike during the Roman period. Artists mixed paint with melted beeswax to brighten the colors.

GREEKS IN POWER
In 332 BC, Alexander the Great took possession of ancient Egypt. Later, the Egyptian city of Alexandria became the leading city in the Greek world.

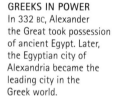

DID YOU KNOW?
Early Christian hermits made their homes in some of the royal tombs at Thebes. They lived in the chapels or offering rooms, not in the actual burial chambers.

SOLDIERS' FOOTWEAR
Archaeologists have found Roman shoes, coins and military equipment at an army outpost in Nubia.

Q: Why was ancient Egypt conquered by invaders?

Ancient China

- Who are the Terra-cotta Warriors?

- When is the Dragon Boat Festival?

- How did ancient chinese people use ox
  and sheep bones to talk to the spirits
  of the dead?

The Middle Kingdom

The civilization of ancient China began about 8,000 years ago, when people settled in areas of the northeast and beside three great rivers—the Yellow River in the north, the Wei River in the northwest and the Yangzi River in the south. They worked the soil with wood and stone tools, grew millet and rice, and raised pigs and dogs. For centuries, the ancient Chinese were enclosed by mountains, deserts and sea, and had little contact with the rest of the world. They developed their own way of life, and called their country "The Middle Kingdom" because they thought it was the center of the universe. Some Chinese leaders were buried in huge underground tombs. Soldiers, convicts and laborers built a wall to keep out northern invaders, and traders from the west traveled to China along the Silk Road.

TAKLAMAKAN DESERT

Wei River

HIMALAYAN MOUNTAINS

N

S

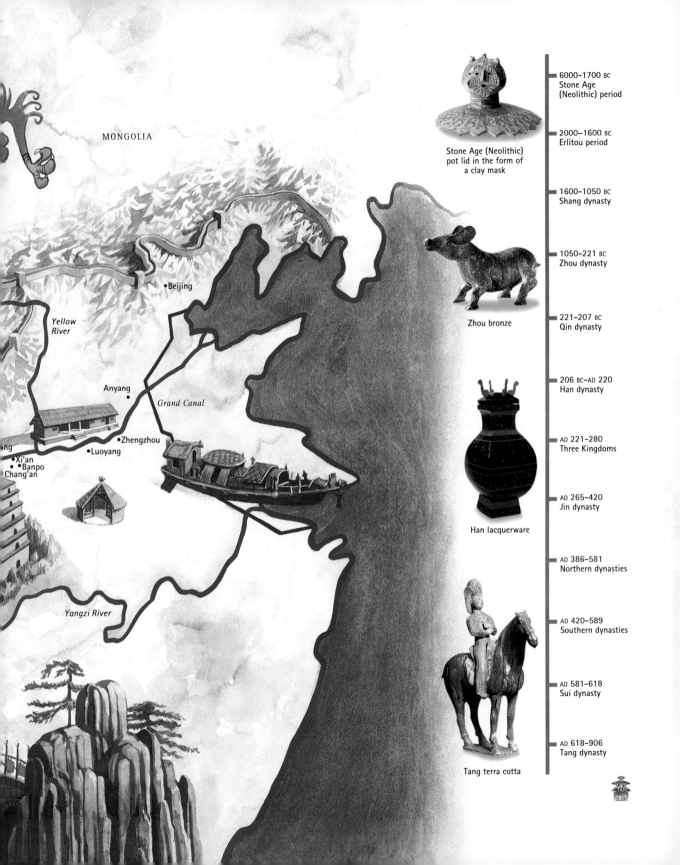

MONGOLIA

Beijing

Yellow River

Anyang

Grand Canal

Zhengzhou

Luoyang

Xi'an
Banpo
Chang'an

Yangzi River

Stone Age (Neolithic)
pot lid in the form of
a clay mask

Zhou bronze

Han lacquerware

Tang terra cotta

6000–1700 BC
Stone Age
(Neolithic) period

2000–1600 BC
Erlitou period

1600–1050 BC
Shang dynasty

1050–221 BC
Zhou dynasty

221–207 BC
Qin dynasty

206 BC–AD 220
Han dynasty

AD 221–280
Three Kingdoms

AD 265–420
Jin dynasty

AD 386–581
Northern dynasties

AD 420–589
Southern dynasties

AD 581–618
Sui dynasty

AD 618–906
Tang dynasty

The Shang Dynasty

I n the Stone Age (Neolithic period), different groups lived in separate communities across the vast land of China. The first dynasty or line of rulers we know about was called the Shang. According to legend, there was a Xia dynasty before them but archaeologists have not yet found any written records from this era. Many things, however, including writing on bronze vessels and oracle bones, survive from Shang times. States fought each other for land until the Shang kings gained control in northern China and set up large cities. Peasants grew food for everyone and craftspeople made tools, weapons, clothing, ornaments and household goods from bronze, silk, jade, clay and other materials. The royal family lived inside a walled palace with their advisers, and diviners who predicted the future. When a king died, servants and animals were sacrificed to go with him to Heaven.

AN AGE OF BRONZE
The large number of containers and other objects made from bronze that survive from the Shang period show advanced methods of production. Artisans adapted ways of working in clay to working in metal. Molten bronze was poured into carved ceramic molds. When the metal cooled, the bronzesmith broke the mold, removed the clay core, and polished the metal surface.

WINE CONTAINER
The Shang liked to drink warm wine. This bronze vessel, made by the clay mold method of casting, was used to hold wine.

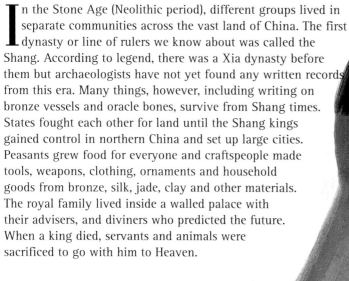

READING THE ORACLE BONES

The Shang believed that spirits of dead ancestors "spoke" to the living through oracle bones. These were the polished shoulder bones of oxen and sheep or the undershells of turtles. A diviner scraped furrows in an oracle bone and inscribed a question on it such as "Is it safe to go on a journey?" Then he scorched the bone and read the cracks that resulted from the heat as the answer to the question.

BURIED BRONZE

China's soil continues to reveal secrets about ancient times. In 1986, brickworkers accidentally uncovered this statue, taller than any man, and life-size heads with strange features.

Discover more in Artists and Artisans

• ANCIENT BEGINNINGS •

The Qin Dynasty

Qin Shi Huangdi.

After more than 800 years of wars and local battles, the powerful Qin people conquered China. The king thanked his ancestors for his success and decided to drop the title wang, which meant "king". He renamed himself Shi (meaning "first") Huangdi (meaning "emperor and divine ruler"). The First Emperor was very important because he unified ancient China by making strict laws, taxing everyone in the country and introducing one script for writing. He commanded his subjects to build roads and canals, and to join existing walls into one long defensive wall. Qin Shi Huangdi did not agree with the teachings of Confucius and other scholars, and ordered their books to be burned. The First Emperor paid magicians, called alchemists, for potions to help him live forever. After his death, his dynasty soon collapsed.

STANDARD COINAGE
Early bronze coins were cast in some unusual shapes. The First Emperor introduced a standard system of money throughout China.

STANDARD WEIGHTS
Qin Shi Huangdi also standardized weights and measures. These included the bronze and terra-cotta cups used for measuring liquids and grains, and the bronze and iron weights that balanced scales.

DID YOU KNOW?
Qin Shi Huangdi, who wanted to live forever, has survived in one way. Qin, pronounced to sound like "chin," gave us the word "China." In a way, the First Emperor's name will never die.

TIGER IN TWO PIECES
An army commander had one part of this model tiger. Messages from the emperor arrived in the second piece to prove that the battle orders were not forged.

PROTECTING THE EMPEROR
In March 1974, well-diggers discovered a silent army guarding the tomb of Qin Shi Huangdi. Pit One contained more than 3,000 life-size foot soldiers and teams of chariot horses.

THE TERRA-COTTA WARRIORS

Qin Shi Huangdi's military companions for eternity march in three pits to the east of his tomb. A fourth pit is empty—the work unfinished at the end of the dynasty in 207 BC. The heads and bodies of the foot soldiers, charioteers and archers (like this one) were made in molds, but no two faces are the same. Some are bearded, others are clean-shaven. Eyes, noses, lips and ears are in many different shapes.

The Han Dynasty

Liu Bang, a government official, gained power and founded the Han dynasty, which lasted for more than 400 years. Han emperors strengthened the Qin system of government and extended ancient China's boundaries. They developed a civil service, based on the teachings of Confucius, to run the empire and keep records in a central place. Scholars who wanted to become government officials had to study very hard. The government organized the salt and iron mines, and state factories began mass-producing objects—from iron and steel farming tools to silk cloth and paper. Han emperors began to control the eastern end of the Silk Road that linked Asia and Europe. Buddhism, one of the most important foreign influences, started to spread throughout ancient China. The Han dynasty finally collapsed after a succession of weak child emperors and droughts and floods.

GILDED BRONZE LEOPARDS
These graceful animals with garnet eyes and inlaid silver spots came from Princess Dou Wan's tomb. They were used as weights.

WATER HIGHWAYS
During the Han era, the people were ordered to build canals to link the cities. These inland waterways made trading, collecting taxes and distributing food during famines much easier. Some families lived on houseboats. Babies often had bamboo floats tied to them until they learned to swim.

AMUSEMENTS FOR THE AFTERLIFE

Acrobats were popular entertainers in ancient China. This tray of tumbling pottery figures was made to amuse the dead in the afterlife.

GOVERNMENT TRANSPORT

Important government officials traveled by horse and carriage. Small models of these were made for their tombs so they would not have to walk in the afterlife.

THE GRAND CANAL

In the Sui period, Emperor Yang decided to link the Yangzi and Yellow rivers by joining new and existing canals. This waterway of 1,550 miles (2,500 km) carried grain and soldiers across his empire. The Grand Canal took more than 30 years to build, and all men 15–50 years of age worked on the project. Every family living nearby also had to send an old man, a woman and a child to the labor force.

Beijing
Grand Canal
Shanghai
China

Q: Why did the Han dynasty collapse?

THE IMPORTANCE OF HORSES

Horses were a sign of great wealth in ancient China. Lifelike pottery models were often buried in the tombs of noblemen.

PATTERNS FROM PERSIA

Chinese artisans copied traditional Persian decoration. The mounted hunter on the side of this jug is copied from a Persian design.

CITY MARKETS

Chang'an was the capital of the Han, Sui and Tang empires. By the Tang era, the busy western market was crammed with warehouses. Foreign merchants brought goods from central and western Asia, India and beyond.

• ANCIENT BEGINNINGS •

The Tang Dynasty

The Tang dynasty ruled ancient China for 300 years. This was a time when art, craft, music and literature further developed, and people called it a golden age. Boundaries expanded again as Tang armies fought successfully against the Koreans in the north, the Vietnamese in the south, and the Tibetans and Turks in the west. The Chinese traded with people from these lands and learned much more about the world beyond China. Buddhism, Confucianism and Daoism were still very important, but traders brought other religious ideas to China along the Silk Road. Visiting craftspeople to the city of Chang'an taught local artisans different ways of making things. Clothing showed the influence of foreign fashions. The wealthy developed a taste for imported foods. They ate dumplings in 24 flavors, tasty sauces, and ice cream made from chilled milk, rice and camphor. Tea, made from the leaves of bushes grown in the warm south, reached northern China's markets during the Tang period, and rich people also enjoyed this new drink.

SKILLED ARTISTS

This is part of a painting on silk called *The Eight Noble Officials*. The figures in their flowing garments show the lively style used by Tang artists.

DID YOU KNOW?

Chang'an was laid out in a square. The four walls had three gates in each wall. Each gate had three gateways—the emperor alone used the central one.

FOREIGN WAYS

During the Tang period, gold and silver became more highly prized than before, and rivaled jade and bronze in value. Persian metalworkers, who fled from their own country and came to live in Chang'an, taught the Chinese more delicate methods of using these precious metals. Tang jewelers began to beat them into thin sheets and to make objects from threads of metal.

STROLLING PLAYERS
Goods for sale were loaded onto the backs of camels and into wagons pulled by oxen. Foreign traders, Chinese merchants and the local crowd enjoyed performances by street acrobats and storytellers.

FOREIGN TONGUES
Among the noisy chatter in the market place, the people of Chang'an heard travelers speaking languages from other parts of the world.

CLOTHED FOR THE AFTERLIFE

As jade seemed to last forever, the ancient Chinese believed this "stone of Heaven" prevented the body from decaying after death. In the Han dynasty, some royal persons were buried in suits made from tiny pieces of jade.

• HEAVEN AND EARTH •

Sons of Heaven

People believed that kings or emperors received heavenly approval to rule. This was called the mandate of Heaven. The mandate was the idea that the country's leader was the Son of Heaven and obtained power from his celestial or heavenly forefathers. Rulers took part in special ceremonies to ask their ancestors to make sure that rain fell at the right time, that it was safe to go on a journey, that hunting was successful and that many other daily events turned out well. An emperor's subjects expected him to be wise, hard-working, unselfish, good and a brilliant military leader. People rebelled against a bad or weak ruler who did not care about their wellbeing, and believed the heavenly spirits showed their displeasure with him through earthquakes, droughts, famine or floods. The mandate was then taken away and given to someone else.

SYMBOLS OF POWER

A number of jade blades have been discovered from Shang times. They were possibly used during ritual ceremonies and perhaps showed the owner's rank or position in society.

"DAUGHTER" OF HEAVEN

The phoenix bird symbolized an empress. Wu Zetian came to power after the death of her husband Gaozong, a weak emperor during the Tang dynasty. Although other women ruled ancient China at various times, Empress Wu Zetian was the only one to claim she had the mandate of Heaven. She chose her advisers from officials who had passed exams instead of favoring people from rich families.

THE EMPEROR'S COURT

In the Tang dynasty, Sons of Heaven ruled the greatest empire in the whole of the ancient world. They displayed their outstanding wealth at court. Gold glittered and silk shone when the emperors exchanged gifts with ambassadors from foreign lands.

COFFIN COVERING
Coffins often nested one inside the other. Sometimes a silk cloak covered the innermost one—perhaps to clothe the dead person on his or her flight to Heaven.

RIDING IN STATE
A model state coach found near the First Emperor's tomb was drawn by four horses harnessed in gold. It had gold furnishings, and doors and windows that opened.

• HEAVEN AND EARTH •

In Life and Death

The ancient Chinese worshipped their ancestors and looked to them for advice on how to manage their daily lives. The ruler spent many hours communicating with his royal forefathers during special ceremonies. They "spoke" to him through oracle bones and other rituals, and advised him on how to run the country. People believed that life continued after death and that they would need their worldly goods when they joined their ancestors in Heaven. The poor went to their graves in cheap coffins with very few possessions. At first, the tombs of the rich contained human sacrifices. In later times, artisans began making copies of servants and attendants in clay, wood or bronze. Burial pits contained many chambers with walls and ceilings decorated to look like the rooms of real houses. Soldiers and mythological creatures guarded the entrance tunnels.

TANG TOMB GUARD
This glazed pottery official shared his duties as a tomb guard with another official, two spirits, two Buddhist guards, two horses, two camels and three grooms.

FIT FOR A PRINCESS
Princess Yongtai died during the Tang dynasty. Her tomb furnishings reflected her high position in life. Some of the walls were covered with exquisite drawings. Jars of wine, food and other household goods made sure she would want for nothing.

A TUNEFUL AFTERLIFE

Musicians often played bells for ancient Chinese lords at solemn rituals or to entertain visitors. This perfectly preserved set of 64 bronze bells mounted on a wooden rack was found in a Zhou tomb. When struck with a wooden stick, each bell produced two notes. The bells in the second row chimed the melody; the larger ones at the bottom provided the accompaniment.

Discover more in The Shang Dynasty

Order in Society

Scholar

Ancient Chinese society was divided into four main classes. The scholar–gentry class was the highest and most esteemed. Scholars were respected above everyone else because they could read and write. Peasants were the next most important class because the country depended on them to produce food. Artisans (people who worked with their hands) used their skills to make things that everyone needed, such as weapons, tools and cooking utensils. The lowest class were merchants. They made nothing, yet often grew rich from trading goods. Laws governed the lifestyle of people in all classes. The size and decoration of officials' houses depended on their rank. An official of the third rank could build a house with five pillars in a row. Officials of the highest importance could add a gate that was three pillars wide.

Peasant

Artisan

A MAGISTRATE'S DUTIES

A district magistrate was a low ranking official in the many-layered government bureaucracy, or organization. He enforced law and order; collected taxes; counted people; registered births, deaths, marriages and property; inspected schools; supervised building programs; and judged court cases.

Merchant

IN ORDER OF IMPORTANCE

Scholars, peasants, artisans and merchants formed the basic social order of ancient China. Soldiers who made a career of being in the army were not highly regarded and did not belong to a class of their own.

BECOMING A PUBLIC SERVANT

Scholars who were interested in the government trained for the imperial civil service. Han Emperor Wu started a university where students learned the teachings of Confucius. These men usually came from wealthy land-owning families, but anyone could take the imperial civil service exams, and sometimes whole villages sponsored a candidate. The few who passed the exams became government officials and magistrates.

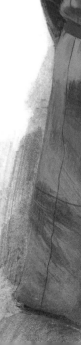

A VERDICT OF GUILTY
When the court believed that evidence collected by investigators or statements from witnesses were enough to prove a person's guilt, the accused was encouraged to confess.

DID YOU KNOW?

Government officials, called censors, had the task of investigating cases of injustice or poor government. They also informed the emperor if they thought he was failing in his duties.

Discover more in The Han Dynasty

NEW WAYS OF FARMING
In the Zhou dynasty, farmers began to use oxen to draw their iron plows. The crop carved along the top of this Han dynasty gravestone is millet.

MODEL GRANARY
Harvested grain was stored in a granary, the most important building on an ancient Chinese farm. This knee-high tomb model of a granary is made from glazed terra cotta.

EARLY HOEING
This stone carving shows the mythical father of Chinese agriculture, Shen Nong, digging with a two-pronged stick.

The Peasant and the Land

Peasant farmers cultivated small plots, and supplied food to the army and to people in the cities. Farmers made the most of the space by cutting terraces into the hill slopes. In spring, there was an important ceremony when the emperor went to the fields to plow the first furrow. Farmers in the north grew barley, wheat and millet to eat, and hemp for clothing. Those in the south planted rice in the soft mud of the flooded paddy fields. Vegetables, such as snow-peas, and lychees and other fruits supplemented these main crops. In some regions, the women raised silkworms. Every able-bodied person in a farming family worked from dawn to dusk. "Agriculture is the foundation of the world," said Han Emperor Wu, but peasants also had to serve in the army and help with government projects such as building walls, canals and dykes.

DEEP FURROWS
Farmers plowed after rain. Hard iron plows, which turned damp soil more easily, replaced softer ones made from wood or bronze. Peasants kept few large animals because they did not want to waste their precious land growing fodder for livestock.

PROBLEMS WITH WATER

In some regions, peasants pedaled irrigation machines to raise water from canals and streams so that their growing crops had regular moisture. The Yellow River spread rich, fertile silt across the valley in good years. But sometimes this great waterway dried to a trickle. At other times, it flooded or changed its course and destroyed whole villages.

DID YOU KNOW?

Everyone had to pay taxes in ancient China. Farmers often paid their taxes in the form of grain or in time spent working for the government.

PAINTED JAR

From earliest times, the ancient Chinese shaped, decorated and fired clay objects. This lidded earthenware vessel was made by a Han potter.

LACQUERED TABLEWARE

Wealthy people used lacquered wooden tableware. Gold, silver and jade banquet vessels were introduced during the Tang dynasty.

FAMILY GATHERINGS

During festivals, a more relaxed atmosphere replaced the strict daily routines of home. Families might go together to visit the graves of ancestors and fathers would spend time with their wives and children.

Family Life

Generations of Chinese families lived together in the same house. Grandfathers, fathers and uncles were considered more important than grandmothers, mothers and aunts, and the birth of a boy was celebrated more than the birth of a girl. The first household rule was that sons and daughters should obey their parents at all times. Children were taught that they must care for their mothers and fathers in sickness and old age. Grandmothers became very important when their husbands died because old people were greatly respected. This was how many women from royal families obtained power in ancient China. When a girl married, she left home and had to obey her husband and parents-in-law. Poor families sometimes sold their daughters to be servants of the rich.

MINIATURE MANSIONS

Clay models from Han tombs tell us that the well-to-do lived in large houses built around spacious courtyards. These mansions had gatehouses and watch towers.

ANCESTOR WORSHIP

Long before Confucius drew up his code of behavior and encouraged ancestor worship, the ancient Chinese believed that the living could "talk" to their forefathers in Heaven. In most family homes, there was an altar for making offerings to the dead, and bronze ritual food vessels were often engraved with family achievements and honors.
In return for this respect, people expected the spirits to protect and look after them.

73

Emperor's hat (mian)

Clothing and Jewelry

DECORATIVE COMB
Women's long hair was arranged in topknots, held in place by hairpins and other ornaments. The pattern on this comb was hammered out by a jeweler.

Lacquered gauze cage hat

Water chestnut kerchief hat

Warrior's helmet

C lothing was a mark of class in ancient China. Fabric textures, colors and decoration, jewelry, headgear and footwear all told something about the wearer's rank and position in society. High-ranking officials dressed in the finest silk for public outings and celebrations, and in less expensive clothes at home. Peasants wore a long, shirtlike garment, made of undyed hemp fiber, which altered little until modern times. During some dynasties, the scholar–gentry class wore jade, gold, silver and brass jewelry, while everyone else had copper and iron accessories. Fashions for the wealthy changed as the years passed. Tang noblewomen, for example, favored the hundred-bird feather skirt, but this was later banned to prevent rare birds from becoming extinct. Tang poems praised women's elaborate make-up. One poem claimed that layers of carefully applied face powder and rouge created "a vision of loveliness."

TANG FASHION
The scholar–gentry class dressed in flowing, silk clothes. Fashionable women wore a long skirt and jacket, topped by a short-sleeved upper garment.

UPTURNED TOES
Some silk brocade shoes, made for the nobility, have survived in the tombs. This fashionable pair belonged to Lady Xin, Marquise of Dai.

Gauze turban (fu tou)

PROPER HEADGEAR
A man's hat completed his outfit, and he would not be seen in public without one. Hat fashions changed through the ages, but they always showed the wearer's occupation and status.

ZHOU BEADS
The craftspeople who made these beads copied designs from Egypt and the Middle East. Layers of colored glass formed a decoration known as the eyes.

TANG FASHION
Men wore loose robes. The wide sleeves were weighted so they hung down without flapping.

THE MAGIC OF MIRRORS
From Han times, polished bronze mirrors were mass-produced. Their beautifully patterned backs represented harmony within the universe. Smaller mirrors, thought to ward off evil spirits, hung from cords at the waist.

FOLLOWERS OF FASHION
Tang princesses wore the latest styles in gowns, shoes and hairdressing. Some design ideas, like the flowers on this dress material, came from countries outside China.

THE IMPORTANCE OF COLOR
Cloth in ancient China was colored with vegetable dyes, and the color of clothing indicated importance. This color coding changed as one dynasty succeeded another. From Sui times onward, only emperors were allowed to wear yellow. Ordinary people had to dress in blue and black. In AD 674, the government made stricter laws to stop people from hiding colored clothing underneath their outer garments. White was for mourning, and children could not wear white while their parents were alive.

75

A Time to Celebrate

Festival days provided a rest from hard daily work. The Spring Festival, which welcomed the new year, lasted for several days. People lit lanterns and exploded bamboo firecrackers. They ate specially prepared vegetable dishes, drank spiced wine, watched street entertainment, and took part in ceremonies to cast out demons. Many festivals dated from Han and Tang times, but Cold Food Day reminded people of Jie Zhi Tui, who served Prince Chong Er loyally during the Spring and Autumn period. When Jie Zhi Tui died in a fire, Chong Er declared an annual festival in his memory. On Cold Food Day, kitchen fires were put out and no cooking was done. Children in the emperor's palace competed to kindle new fire by twirling sticks on wooden boards for a prize of three rolls of silk cloth and a lacquered bowl. Some ancient festivals are still important in China today.

LAST DROPS
Ladles, shaped from lacquered wood, were used to scoop wine from deep storage jars. The ancient Chinese made wine from rice.

MUSICAL ACCOMPANIMENT
Musicians performed at banquets and solemn ceremonies. In this group, three players pluck zithers with 25 strings. The other two blow bamboo mouth organs.

TANG TABLEWARE
In Tang times, metalsmiths began to hammer out sheets of gold and silver to make cups and bowls. Banquet tables were set with beautifully shaped vessels decorated with graceful designs.

DRAGON BOAT FESTIVAL

The Dragon Boat Festival, held on the fifth day of the fifth month, is still celebrated today. Rowing boats, decorated at prow and stern to look like dragons, race on lakes and rivers as part of the celebrations. Other craft took to the water in ancient times. Paintings show people enjoying the day in pleasure boats with an upper and lower deck.

Discover more in In Life and Death

Medical Practice

Confucius taught that the body was a gift from your parents. It was considered disrespectful not to take care of yourself. The ancient Chinese believed that exercising and eating herbs promoted good health. One Han physician worked out the Five Animal Exercises based on the movements of tigers, deer, apes, bears and cranes. If the forces of Yin and Yang became unbalanced in the body, a person fell sick. Physicians used three main treatments—herbal cures, acupuncture and moxibustion. Moxibustion involved burning a small amount of a dried herb called moxa on an acupuncture point to spread a healing warmth through the body. Ancient Chinese studies of medicine are the oldest in the world. By Tang times, doctors had to pass regular exams to prove their knowledge. Medicine was considered honorable work for scholars, and was one of the few professions open to women.

DID YOU KNOW?

Ancient Chinese doctors discovered the body's natural 24-hour cycle, which we call the circadian rhythm. This cycle governs our times of waking and sleeping and our moods during the day.

THE POWER OF ACUPUNCTURE

Ancient Chinese physicians thought that life-giving energy flowed along 12 lines in the body called meridians. Doctors were able to ease pain and treat certain illnesses by sticking acupuncture needles just below the skin at points along these meridians.

78

TO LIVE FOREVER

Followers of the Daoist religion believed they could find an elixir of life made from herbs and extracts of metals. This powerful mixture would allow people to live forever. Alchemists searched for a magic process that would turn base metals into gold fluid. Many elixirs, however, contained small quantities of deadly poisons such as mercury and arsenic.

Star anise

Ginseng

Chinese parsley (coriander)

Garlic

AN ANCIENT WORKOUT
These fragments are part of a chart painted on silk. It was found in a Han tomb and presented more than 40 exercises to keep the body in good shape.

GUARDIANS OF THE HOURS
The ancient Chinese believed that spirits guarded the hours of the day. This Han tile shows the Guardian of Midnight on duty from 11 pm to 1 am.

Discover more in Family Life

FIRST EDITION
Probably the earliest complete printed book to survive is a Buddhist text called *The Diamond Sutra*, printed in AD 868. It is in the form of a scroll nearly 20 ft (6 m) long.

SIGNED WITH A SEAL
Seals, usually impressed into red ink paste, frequently replaced signatures. The seals had from one to dozens of characters, and were carved or molded from bronze, silver, stone, horn, wood or jade.

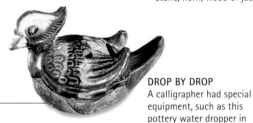

DROP BY DROP
A calligrapher had special equipment, such as this pottery water dropper in the shape of a duck.

JADE BRUSH REST
Brush rests, often designed in animal forms, stopped wet brushes from rolling when the calligrapher was not using them.

• DISCOVERY, ART AND INVENTION •

Writing and Printing

Writing began to develop very early in ancient China. Early inscriptions were written on oracle bones and then on bronze ritual vessels. Bamboo strips, wooden tablets and pieces of silk were also used as writing materials. In about AD 105, government official Cai Lun suggested that pulping bark, roots, rags and old fishnets would improve the quality of paper, which had been invented several centuries before. This process was one of the most important discoveries of all time. In the Tang era, impressions from seals and the making of ink rubbings of engraved stone tablets led to the idea of printing. Text was written on fine paper and pasted, front side down, onto a wooden block. The printer cut away the background to leave raised characters. He then inked the surface of the block and pressed paper sheets against it to produce an image that was the right way up.

KEEPING THE RECORDS
Before people had paper, they wrote on bamboo, cutting the characters into the thin strips of wood from top to bottom. Many government records survive in this form.

CHINESE CHARACTERS

Chinese writing uses symbols for words and phrases and is read vertically (down and up) rather than horizontally (side to side). Some characters have up to 26 brushstrokes, which must be drawn in the correct order. Qin Shi Huangdi ordered a standard form of writing so that imperial commands could be read throughout the country. This script has not changed much until recent times.

口 mouth

日 sun

月 moon

王 ruler, king

THE ART OF CALLIGRAPHY

Ancient Chinese calligraphers wrote with brushes made from animal hairs, tied together with fine silk threads and glued in bamboo tubes. Calligraphers mixed their ink by rubbing a solid ink stick with drops of water on an ink stone.

Artists and Artisans

Painting was an important art form that developed alongside calligraphy. Artists had to perfect their brushstrokes, use a variety of colors, produce well-balanced compositions and represent their subject matter accurately. From the fourth century AD, painters were often recognized by name, but artisans who worked in teams usually remained anonymous. They made bronze, jade, clay and other materials into beautiful objects for religious rituals and household purposes, and fashioned thousands of tomb models of almost everything to do with daily life. Once the process of iron casting was developed, governments set up iron foundries to mass-produce agricultural tools and military weapons. Other state factories turned out lacquerware and silk cloth.

In the ninth century AD, an Arab author, Jahiz of Basra, commented that the Turks were the greatest soldiers, the Persians the best kings and the Chinese the most gifted of all craftspeople.

THE ART OF LACQUER
Sap from the lacquer tree is the oldest industrial plastic known to humans. Wood, bamboo or cloth utensils, coated with many thin layers of lacquer, can withstand the heat of cooking. The ancient Chinese colored lacquer black, red, brown, yellow, gold and green.

JADE DRAGON
The ancient Chinese valued jade, the "Stone of Heaven," above all other materials. Dragons, which were believed to have special powers, appeared frequently in their art.

TURNING THE PAGE
Books with bound pages took the place of scrolls in ancient China during the Tang dynasty. By this time, more women were learning to read.

WINE VESSEL
Birds with long plumes began appearing as decoration on bronze containers made in the middle Western Zhou period.

PATTERNED BOXES

Han potters were the first to glaze with lead. By the Tang period, lead-glazed ceramics were more boldly decorated. Potters often chose bright colors.

PEOPLE OF JADE

Hard jade stone was difficult to work. It was shaped with bamboo drills tipped with bronze, rubbed smooth with abrasive rock sand, and buffed on wood and leather polishing wheels.

BRONZE STATUE

Bronze, a mixture of copper, tin and sometimes lead, lasts forever. Silk and wood often rots to dust.

LACQUER ON THE LINE

Wealthy Chinese babies were fed using lacquer spoons and lacquer bowls. Wealthy Chinese people were buried in lacquer coffins. Artisans on production lines turned out many thousands of costly lacquer goods. This wine cup, surviving from the Han dynasty, is inscribed with the names of eight artisans and five supervisory officials who helped to produce the vessel.

Arched bridge
Engineer Li Chun designed an arched bridge in AD 610. It was stronger and took less stone to build than other bridges.

Horsepower
The Han invented trace (or breast) harnesses for horses. These replaced choking throat straps and greatly increased the animals' pulling power.

• DISCOVERY, ART AND INVENTION •

New Ideas

The ancient Chinese were always looking for practical ways to solve problems. Farmers hung bags of killer ants in their orchards to eat the insect pests that would otherwise have destroyed the mandarin orange crop. Ancient Chinese inventors were way ahead of the rest of the world. They developed wheelbarrows, for example, about 1,300 years before Europeans copied the idea. Their inventions of paper, printing, the compass and gunpowder have probably had more impact on the world than anything else that has ever been invented. The earliest compass, called a "south-pointing fish," consisted of a wooden fish containing a piece of metal floating in a bowl of water. Gunpowder, made from saltpeter, sulfur and charcoal, was used by alchemists and physicians long before it was used for weapons. Other notable inventions included matches, the game of chess and mechanical clocks.

Rudder
Ancient Chinese ships had rudders, essential for steering properly, by the first century AD. European navigators began to use rudders around AD 1180.

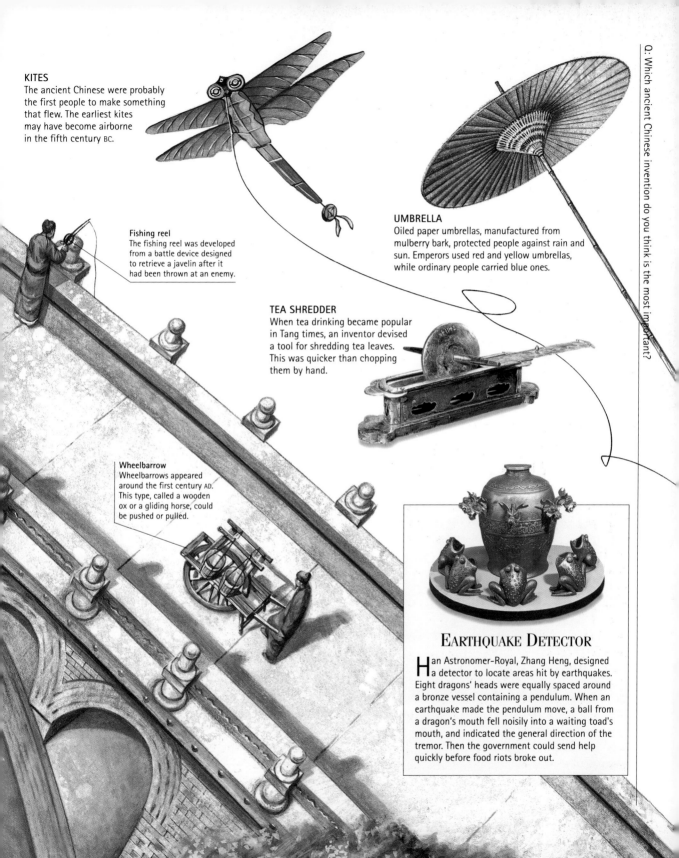

KITES

The ancient Chinese were probably the first people to make something that flew. The earliest kites may have become airborne in the fifth century BC.

Fishing reel
The fishing reel was developed from a battle device designed to retrieve a javelin after it had been thrown at an enemy.

UMBRELLA

Oiled paper umbrellas, manufactured from mulberry bark, protected people against rain and sun. Emperors used red and yellow umbrellas, while ordinary people carried blue ones.

TEA SHREDDER

When tea drinking became popular in Tang times, an inventor devised a tool for shredding tea leaves. This was quicker than chopping them by hand.

Wheelbarrow
Wheelbarrows appeared around the first century AD. This type, called a wooden ox or a gliding horse, could be pushed or pulled.

EARTHQUAKE DETECTOR

Han Astronomer-Royal, Zhang Heng, designed a detector to locate areas hit by earthquakes. Eight dragons' heads were equally spaced around a bronze vessel containing a pendulum. When an earthquake made the pendulum move, a ball from a dragon's mouth fell noisily into a waiting toad's mouth, and indicated the general direction of the tremor. Then the government could send help quickly before food riots broke out.

Ancient Greece

- When and where did the ancient Olympic games begin?

- What could a dinner guest expect to eat at a banquet in ancient Greece?

- What popular game used the ankle joints of goats or sheep?

MACEDONIA

ITALY

Mount Olympus ▲

IONIAN SEA

Thermopylae •

Delphi •

Thebes •

Marathon •

• Athens

Corinth •

• Olympia

Sparta •

MEDITERRANEAN SEA

• THE GREEK WORLD •

A Seafaring People

T he ancient Greek world took shape between 3200 and 1100 BC. This was during the Bronze Age when people first began melting copper with tin to make bronze. Island communities occupied the Cyclades and Crete, and the Mycenaean civilization lived on mountainous mainland Greece. From the beginning, the ancient Greeks farmed the narrow valleys and coastal plains, wherever there was good soil and a river or a freshwater spring. Through the centuries, they cut trees from the mountain slopes for firewood and to build ships. They used ships more than any other means of transport, sailing the seas to trade, to go to war and to settle new places. Ancient Greek legends told of brave seafarers who survived dangerous voyages. Greece's boundaries expanded greatly from around 700 BC onward. Art and ideas developed strongly, and during the Hellenistic Age, the Greek way of life spread to many other countries.

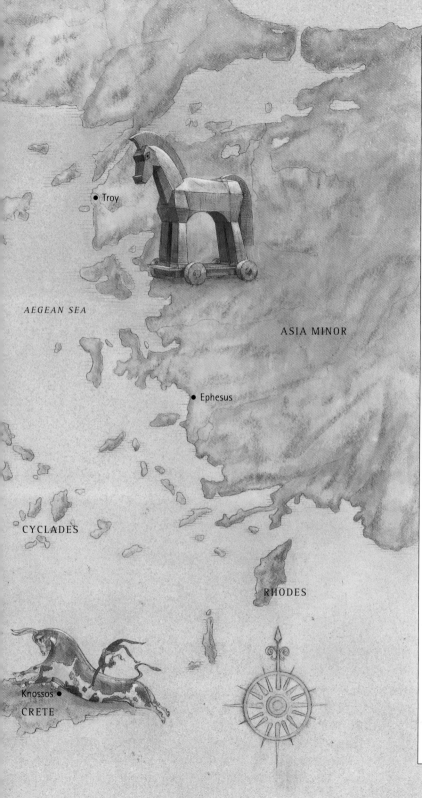

AEGEAN SEA

Troy

ASIA MINOR

Ephesus

CYCLADES

RHODES

Knossos

CRETE

AGES OF ANCIENT GREECE

CYCLADIC CIVILIZATION
3200–1100 BC
A Cycladic figurine of a harp player made from marble.

MINOAN CIVILIZATION
3200–1100 BC

MYCENAEAN CIVILIZATION
1600–1100 BC
A Mycenaean pottery cup decorated with a pattern of cuttlefish.

DARK AGE AND GEOMETRIC PERIOD
1100–700 BC

ARCHAIC PERIOD
700–480 BC
This Archaic bronze griffin's head was once attached to a large cooking pot.

CLASSICAL PERIOD
480–323 BC
A Classical red-figure vase showing Odysseus meeting a swineherd.

HELLENISTIC AGE
323–31 BC
A Hellenistic terracotta figure of the god Eros.

Discover more in End of an Empire

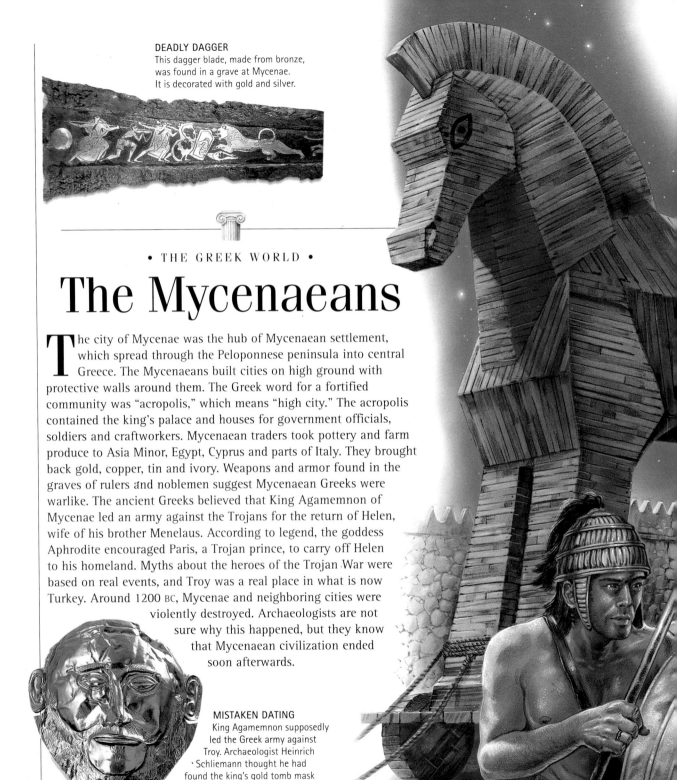

DEADLY DAGGER
This dagger blade, made from bronze, was found in a grave at Mycenae. It is decorated with gold and silver.

The Mycenaeans

The city of Mycenae was the hub of Mycenaean settlement, which spread through the Peloponnese peninsula into central Greece. The Mycenaeans built cities on high ground with protective walls around them. The Greek word for a fortified community was "acropolis," which means "high city." The acropolis contained the king's palace and houses for government officials, soldiers and craftworkers. Mycenaean traders took pottery and farm produce to Asia Minor, Egypt, Cyprus and parts of Italy. They brought back gold, copper, tin and ivory. Weapons and armor found in the graves of rulers and noblemen suggest Mycenaean Greeks were warlike. The ancient Greeks believed that King Agamemnon of Mycenae led an army against the Trojans for the return of Helen, wife of his brother Menelaus. According to legend, the goddess Aphrodite encouraged Paris, a Trojan prince, to carry off Helen to his homeland. Myths about the heroes of the Trojan War were based on real events, and Troy was a real place in what is now Turkey. Around 1200 BC, Mycenae and neighboring cities were violently destroyed. Archaeologists are not sure why this happened, but they know that Mycenaean civilization ended soon afterwards.

MISTAKEN DATING
King Agamemnon supposedly led the Greek army against Troy. Archaeologist Heinrich Schliemann thought he had found the king's gold tomb mask at Mycenae. But this mask was made long before the Trojan War.

90

GIFT HORSE

After fighting the Trojans for ten years, the Greeks left a huge wooden horse outside Troy's walls and sailed away. The curious Trojans wheeled the statue into the city. That night, Greek soldiers hiding inside the hollow horse crept out and opened the gates. Their army, which had returned silently, entered Troy and defeated the Trojans.

SEARCHING FOR TROY

As a small boy, Heinrich Schliemann read about the Trojan War in Homer's *Iliad* and he vowed to find Troy. In 1870, relying on details from Homer's poem, Schliemann began to unearth a city at Hissarlik in Turkey. He discovered jewelry that he believed had belonged to Troy's King Priam. Nine cities lying on top of one another have since been found at Hissarlik. The city in the sixth layer is most likely to have been Troy.

Sophie Schliemann wearing jewelry excavated by her husband.

FRESCO AT MYCENAE

Frescoes are pictures painted on the walls of buildings while the plaster is still wet. These donkey-headed demons survive from the thirteenth century BC.

DID YOU KNOW?

Homer, a poet who lived in the eighth century BC, retold well-known Mycenaean legends in the *Iliad* and *Odyssey*. These long poems were possibly not written down until after Homer died.

MARINE THEME

The tentacles of an octopus writhe around this jar. Sea creatures, an important source of food, were popular in designs on Mycenaean pottery.

LIONS ON GUARD

The Lion Gate, named for the animals carved above it, was the main entrance to Mycenae. It was built about 1250 BC when the enormous stone city walls were increased in size.

GRIFFIN ON GUARD
Greek craftworkers sometimes learned new skills from their neighbors. This griffin's head was made by bronze hollow casting, a method used in Asia Minor.

Settling New Lands

When the Mycenaean civilization ended, troubled times fell on ancient Greece. This period, now called the Dark Age, lasted about 400 years. It is thought that people forgot how to write because no writing has been found from this era. When food became scarce some people left their homeland to find new places to settle. They migrated to the coast of Asia Minor, stopping off at the Aegean Islands on the way. By the eighth century BC, Greece had recovered, but the growing population was overcrowding the mainland. Greek colonies spread around the Black Sea to the northeast, and west to southern Italy, and as far as France and Spain. Most colonies became farming communities, but a few were set up as trading posts. Successful settlements sent supplies back to Greece to relieve shortages there. The Black Sea ports exchanged grain and timber for wine, olive oil and honey.

MINTED TO MATCH
Early silver coins from some southern Italian colonies had a raised design on one side and the reverse design on the other. These coins were very difficult to make.

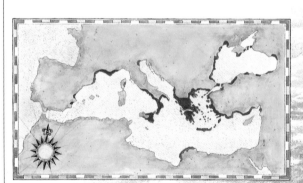

A RING OF COLONIES
The red on this map shows where the Greeks settled around the edges of the seas. Settlers looked for a natural harbor, good soil and a climate similar to their homeland.

RICHES FROM THE COLONIES
This scepter is covered in gold, wrapped in gold wire, and crowned with gold acanthus leaves. It was made in Taranto, a wealthy colony in southern Italy.

TIES WITH HOME
Settlers built new cities to look like those they had left behind. There was a central meeting place and a temple on the highest ground for their special god or goddess.

ON THE RUN
Nike was the winged goddess of victory. This bronze statue might once have adorned the rim of a bowl in southern Italy.

SAFE HARBOR
Colonies were usually established beside the sea. Settlements developed their own systems of government but kept in touch with their homeland. Ships sailed to and fro carrying supplies and news.

THE ORACLE OF DELPHI

Leaders of colonizing expeditions always consulted a priest in Apollo's temple at Delphi about where to settle. The buildings at the sacred site of Delphi on the steep slopes of Mount Parnassus were a center of ancient Greek religious life. The vase below shows a procession on its way to visit Apollo's shrine. People believed Apollo answered questions about the future through his priestesses who spoke while in trances. Priests explained these answers, known as oracles. Oracles could often be understood in more than one way. So, whatever happened, the hearer would think that the oracle had come true.

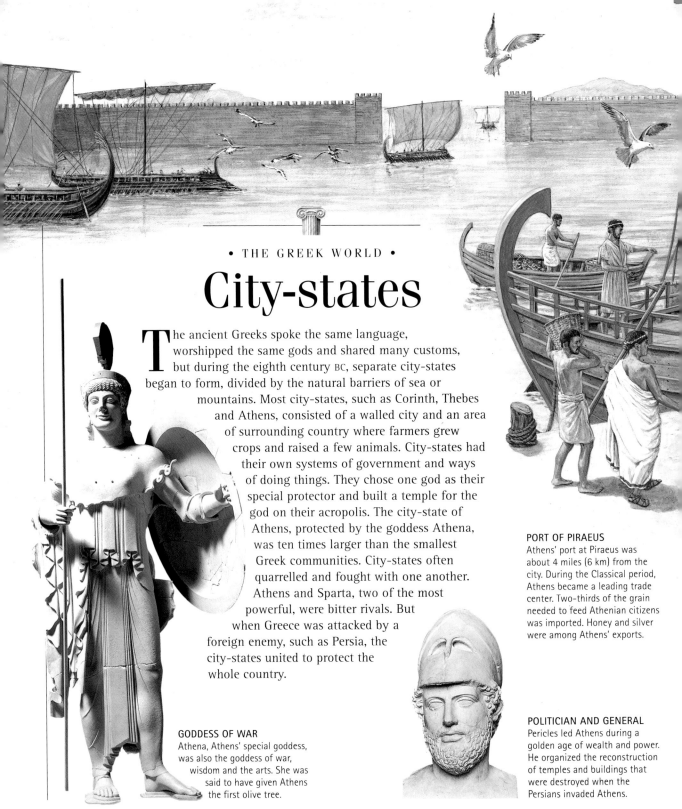

City-states

The ancient Greeks spoke the same language, worshipped the same gods and shared many customs, but during the eighth century BC, separate city-states began to form, divided by the natural barriers of sea or mountains. Most city-states, such as Corinth, Thebes and Athens, consisted of a walled city and an area of surrounding country where farmers grew crops and raised a few animals. City-states had their own systems of government and ways of doing things. They chose one god as their special protector and built a temple for the god on their acropolis. The city-state of Athens, protected by the goddess Athena, was ten times larger than the smallest Greek communities. City-states often quarrelled and fought with one another. Athens and Sparta, two of the most powerful, were bitter rivals. But when Greece was attacked by a foreign enemy, such as Persia, the city-states united to protect the whole country.

PORT OF PIRAEUS
Athens' port at Piraeus was about 4 miles (6 km) from the city. During the Classical period, Athens became a leading trade center. Two-thirds of the grain needed to feed Athenian citizens was imported. Honey and silver were among Athens' exports.

GODDESS OF WAR
Athena, Athens' special goddess, was also the goddess of war, wisdom and the arts. She was said to have given Athens the first olive tree.

POLITICIAN AND GENERAL
Pericles led Athens during a golden age of wealth and power. He organized the reconstruction of temples and buildings that were destroyed when the Persians invaded Athens.

LIVING IN SPARTA

The city-state of Sparta was enclosed by a mountain range, so it did not need protective walls. It was the only city-state to keep a permanent army, and Spartan soldiers were recognized as the best in ancient Greece. All Spartan children belonged to the state and boys began their tough military training at the age of seven. Even when they married, Spartan men still lived in army barracks.

TEST OF TIME

This painting from the nineteenth century shows how well some of the temples on Athens' acropolis survived through the centuries.

Discover more in Building in Stone

WATER CLOCK
In court, speakers were timed by a water clock. Their time was up when all the water from the upper pot had run into the lower one.

SELECTING A JURY
Citizens fit their names into the slots of an allotment machine. A fragment of one is shown here. Colored balls dropped beside the rows of names to show the jurors for that day.

• THE GREEK WORLD •

Government and the Law

In early times, groups of rich landowners ran the city-states, but sometimes one leader, called a tyrant, seized power. Tyrants usually ruled fairly, but some were cruel and unjust. Athens introduced a system of government called democracy. Many other city-states developed the same system. We know most about the way Athens was organized from surviving evidence. In Athens, democracy allowed every citizen to have a say in state affairs. But only men who were born in the city-state and were not slaves could become citizens. A council of 500 citizens, drawn annually in a lottery, suggested new laws and policies. Citizens voted at the assembly to accept, change or reject these suggestions. Juries of more than 200 citizens tried most Athenian law cases. Jurors were also chosen by lot. There were no lawyers, and only citizens could speak in court.

TRIAL BY JURY
After a trial, jury members cast their verdicts with bronze discs. They used tokens with solid centers to show the accused was innocent, and tokens with hollow centers to show the accused was guilty.

PUBLIC SPEAKER
Oratory is the art of making public speeches. Aeschines, the famous Athenian orator, started a school in Rhodes for speech makers.

96

POINTS OF VIEW
Any Athenian citizen, rich or poor, could explain his point of view to the assembly. At least 6,000 citizens had to be present before a meeting could begin. Once all opinions about a matter had been heard, the whole assembly voted on it.

LOSING THE VOTE

The Athenians had a way of getting rid of politicians they did not trust. Once a year, assembly members could vote against the ones they disliked. Citizens wrote the names of unpopular politicians on pieces of pottery called ostraca. A man who received more than 6,000 votes had to leave Athens for ten years. This method of exiling people was called ostracism. Arissteides and Kimon, named on these fragments, were both ostracized.

ARISSTEIDES
LVSIMATO

KIMON
MIATAIADO

On Mount Olympus

The top of Mount Olympus, the highest mountain on mainland Greece, is often hidden by clouds. The ancient Greeks imagined that gods and goddesses, who looked and behaved like humans, lived on the mountain. However, these supernatural beings drank nectar and ate ambrosia, which made them immortal—they could not grow old or die. The people believed the gods and goddesses controlled events in life and nature, and had power to shape the future. Apollo made the sun rise and set. Hermes cared for travelers and led souls to the Underworld. Zeus, the king of the gods, roared with thunder and threw lightning bolts when he was angry. Poseidon whipped up storms at sea or caused earthquakes. Every village had its own guardian god or goddess although some were not important enough to live on Mount Olympus. The Greeks built temples for their deities and organized animal sacrifices, processions, plays and games to please them.

THINGS FROM THE PAST
Sometimes, archaeologists find it difficult to identify the things they find. This statue is thought to be the goddess Hera.

Zeus
God of the sky and thunder.

Head of Zeus

Poseidon
God of earthquakes, the sea, horses and bulls.

Hestia
Goddess of the family and the hearth.

Hermes
Messenger of the gods and protector of travelers.

Aphrodite
Goddess of love and beauty.

Athena
Goddess of wisdom, art and war.

Ares
God of war.

THE GODDESS ARTEMIS

This terracotta figurine of Artemis dates from the Hellenistic Age. It was made in Myrina, a Greek city in Asia Minor.

THE GODDESS APHRODITE

According to one legend, beautiful Aphrodite was born from sea foam. Here, her attendants are helping her to rise from the water.

PAN, A NATURE SPIRIT

Country people worshipped nature spirits. Pan, protector of shepherds and their flocks, was the best known of these lesser supernatural beings. Pan was a satyr—half man, half goat. Although his upper body was human, his face was goatlike and he had horns. Pan wandered across lonely mountain tops playing his panpipes—a wind instrument made from seven hollow reeds, graded in length and bound together.

GODDESS WITHOUT A NAME

The early Mycenaeans worshipped some deities that later Greeks placed on Mount Olympus. Mycenaean sites also contained terracotta images of unknown gods and goddesses, such as this one.

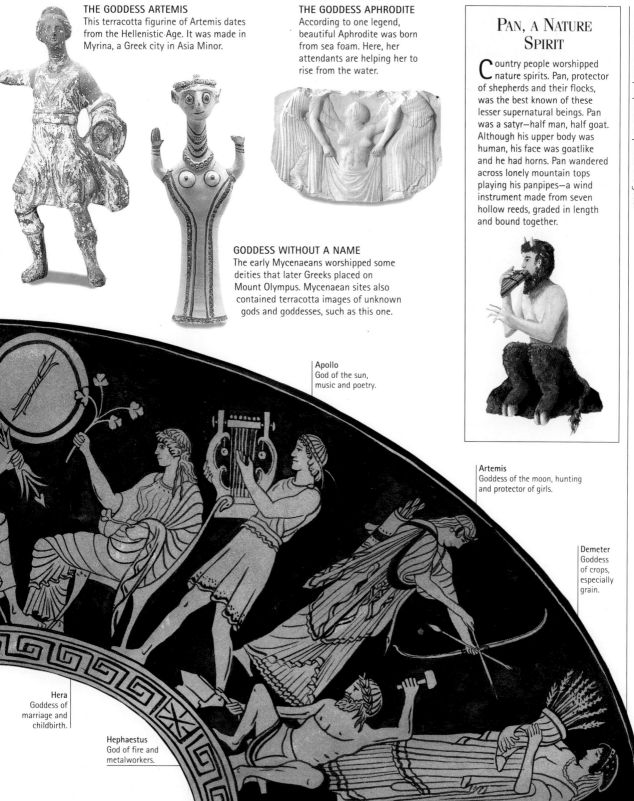

Apollo
God of the sun, music and poetry.

Artemis
Goddess of the moon, hunting and protector of girls.

Demeter
Goddess of crops, especially grain.

Hera
Goddess of marriage and childbirth.

Hephaestus
God of fire and metalworkers.

CHILDREN'S TOYS
Spinning tops and dolls were made from terra-cotta—a mixture of clay and sand. The writing on the pottery baby's bottle says, "drink, don't drop!"

• LIVING IN ANCIENT GREECE •

In the Home

Houses had stone foundations, mud-brick walls and roofs of pottery tiles. Small, high windows kept out heat and burglars. Doors and shutters were made of wood. The central open courtyard contained an altar where the family worshipped their gods. Some courtyards also had a well, but water was usually fetched from public fountains. Women ran the household with the help of slaves. In ancient Greece, women had to obey their fathers, husbands, brothers or sons. A father could abandon his newborn child. He might do this if the baby was sickly, but healthy infant girls were also abandoned sometimes. Most women married at 15, while men married at 30 or more. The father chose his daughter's husband and gave the bridegroom money or valuables to save for his wife in case he wanted a divorce or died before she did. Sometimes, a bride met her husband for the first time on the day she was married.

WOMEN'S QUARTERS
Men and women had separate quarters. Women wove cloth in the loom room.

MEN'S QUARTERS
The head of the household entertained guests in a dining room furnished with couches.

LOOM DUTIES
The women of the family produced a great amount of cloth for household furnishings and clothing. Girls learned how to spin and weave from their mothers.

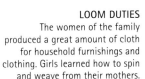

DID YOU KNOW?
Children stopped being infants at the age of three. In Athens, at a spring festival, they were given miniature wine jugs, such as this, to mark the end of their babyhood.

GETTING MARRIED

On her wedding day, a bride bathed in sacred spring water and dressed in white. That night, the bridegroom and his friends came to fetch her. The very wealthy had horse-drawn chariots, while others had carts or walked. At the bridegroom's home, the couple knelt at the altar and his family showered them with nuts, dried fruit and sweets before they went to the bridal chamber. The next day, the two families celebrated at the husband's house.

IN THE KITCHEN
Slaves baked bread in a
pottery oven and cooked food on
an open fire. The smoke escaped
through a hole in the roof.

OUT TO PLAY
Girls played
knucklebones using
the ankle joints of
goats or sheep. But
the day before they
married, girls had
to leave all their
playthings at the
temple of Artemis.

HOME FURNISHINGS
Couches, tables, stools,
chairs, beds and storage chests
were made from wood and bronze.
Oil-burning lamps provided light. Wealthy
people had bathrooms in their homes and
plenty of slaves to fill the tubs with water.

Discover more in Eating and Drinking

ΑΒΓΔΕΖΗΘΙΚΛΜΝΞΟΠΡΣΤ

• LIVING IN ANCIENT GREECE •

Writing and Education

E ducation in ancient Greece was not free. Only the sons of wealthy citizens could afford to go to school, where they attended classes from about the age of seven. The sons of poorer citizens learned their father's trade. At 18, youths were trained to fight so they were prepared to go to war when necessary. Some girls were taught to read and write at home, but lessons in housework were considered much more important. One writer even said that sending a girl to school would be like "giving extra poison to a dangerous snake!" In Sparta, education was much tougher than elsewhere in Greece. When they were seven, Spartan boys went to board in army barracks. They were given so little to eat that they had to steal food. This was supposed to teach them to be cunning soldiers. Spartan girls attended gymnastics, dancing, music and singing lessons.

AT SCHOOL
Boys learned reading, writing and arithmetic. Students wrote with pointed sticks on wooden tablets covered in soft wax. Mistakes could be rubbed out easily. Athletics and dancing were also important lessons.

INSPIRED BY MUSES
This stone carving shows three of the nine Muses, the goddesses of arts and science. They were thought to inspire poets, playwrights, musicians, dancers and astronomers.

102

GREEK ALPHABET
The word alphabet comes from two Greek letters—alpha and beta. There were 24 letters in the ancient Greek alphabet.

THE DEVELOPMENT OF WRITING

The Linear B script on these clay tablets was adapted by the Mycenaeans from Minoan Linear A script. It was forgotten during the Dark Age. Greeks began to write again in the eighth century BC. They borrowed an alphabet from the Near Eastern Phoenicians and altered it slightly. Phoenicians wrote from right to left but the Greeks eventually reversed this direction. Early Greeks wrote only in capitals with no spaces between words and no punctuation.

APOLLO AND THE MUSE
Apollo, god of music and poetry, is shown here talking to a Muse. Apollo worked closely with the nine goddesses.

MUSIC LESSON
Boys learned to play the lyre and pipes from a teacher called a kitharistes. This teacher also taught poetry and students had to memorize very long poems.

PIPES AND LYRES
Music lessons, like this one painted on a water vase, were often attended by several students. It seems that dogs and pet cheetahs were also welcome.

Dressing for the Climate

Summers in ancient Greece were hot and dry. Winters were wet with chilly north winds. The poet Hesiod said that winter gales were cold enough to "skin an ox." People wore clothing made from rectangular pieces of material wrapped around the body in soft folds. They covered their summer garments with warm cloaks in winter. Statues and paintings on vases show that fashions changed slowly. The women of the household spun sheep's fleeces into fine woolen thread and flax fibers into linen. They dyed the yarns in bright colors and sometimes wove a contrasting color or a pattern into the edge of the fabric. Imported silk cloth was very costly. Cotton was introduced into Greece after Alexander the Great reached India. The ancient Greeks went barefoot or wore sandals, shoes or boots. Wealthy men and women owned fine jewelry. Slaves in the mines and stone quarries, who were at the poorer end of the social scale, wore only loincloths.

DID YOU KNOW?

Suntans were unfashionable in ancient Greece. In summer, said Hesiod, "the sun scorches head and knees." Both men and women wore broad-brimmed hats to protect their faces when they went outdoors.

SHOULDER PINS
These bronze dress pins came from mainland Boeotia. They measure about 18 in (45 cm) in length.

MIRROR IMAGE
Containers of sweet-smelling oils often pictured lifelike figures on a background of white clay. Greek women cared greatly about face make-up and hairstyles.

WOMEN'S WEAR
Women wore a long tunic made of wool or linen, fastened on the shoulders with brooches or large pins and tied at the waist and sometimes at the hips. Wraps ranged from thin shawls to heavy traveling cloaks.

SPINNING AND WEAVING

Women and girls spent many hours weaving fabric from local sheep's wool. They made clothing for the household, wall hangings, and covers and cushions for wooden furniture. Raw wool had to be spun into thread before it could be woven into material. The woman pictured on the vase (left) is spinning with tools called a distaff and a spindle. In her left hand she holds the distaff wrapped in unspun wool. She pulls out the wool with her right hand and twists it slowly to form thread. The thread is fed onto the spindle, which is weighted to keep it steady.

JEWELRY FROM RHODES

This chest ornament belonged to a rich man. He wore it by pinning the rosettes to his shoulders. The seven gold plaques show winged goddesses and lions. Pomegranates hang beneath them.

MENSWEAR

Men and boys usually wore thigh-length tunics; old men favored longer hemlines. Winter cloaks were often draped to leave one shoulder bare.

ELEGANT FOLDS

Women wore two main tunic styles—folded over at the top (below left) and usually made from wool, or fastened on the shoulders in several places (below right) and usually made from linen.

105

DID YOU KNOW?
The Greeks called foreigners "barbarians" because they could not understand what these people said. They thought all words in unknown languages sounded like "bar-bar."

HARD AS IRON
During the Greek Dark Age, people learned to forge iron. They began to make sickles and other farm tools out of this strong metal.

DAILY NEEDS
Women ground barley to make porridge, gruel and bread. They baked loaves in ovens. Wheat flour was more expensive and bought only by the wealthy.

METAL WORKING
Metal ores were heated in furnaces. Workers took the red-hot ore from the fire with tongs. They hammered it into shape while it was soft.

Making a Living

Many ancient Greeks worked hard. Fishermen and country folk provided food, such as sea creatures, olive oil, wine, grain, fruit, vegetables and honey, for people who lived in the towns. Farmers kept sheep, goats, pigs, poultry, donkeys and cattle, but only people in northern mainland Greece had enough pasture to breed horses. City people earned their living from making or selling things, such as leather goods, furniture, pots, tools, weapons and jewelry. It was unusual for well-born women to work outside the home, but some were priestesses in the temples. Low-born women became midwives, shopkeepers, dancers or musicians. Citizens who could afford to buy slaves or hire laborers looked down on those who had to work for a living. Rich men owned farms or ran silver mines and lived off the profits. They took part in public affairs, fought in the army when required, and paid high state taxes.

MAKING WINE

Grapes were picked when they ripened in September. A few bunches were set aside for eating. The rest were tipped into huge vats and stamped on to squeeze out the juice. This was poured into jars and left to ferment into wine.

SERVED BY SLAVES

Slaves did much of the work in ancient Greece. They were often prisoners of war or pirates' captives and were bought and sold in the markets. Many were educated. The children of slaves also became slaves. Sometimes slave traders reared abandoned babies to sell later. Household servants were usually treated well. A few even saved their tiny wages and bought their freedom. But slaves in the silver mines and stone quarries worked in terrible conditions.

OLIVE HARVEST

The scene on this vase shows men beating the ripe olives from the lower branches of olive trees with poles. Boys climbed the trees to reach the higher fruit.

Discover more in Sickness and Health

• LIVING IN ANCIENT GREECE •

Meeting Place

Every city had a central open space for meetings and markets. It was called the "agora." Men frequently did the shopping in ancient Greece and slaves carried the purchases. The agora must have been a noisy place, with customers jostling for attention at the covered stalls. Donkeys trotted to market bearing large loads of country produce. Strong smells mingled with fragrant, spicy odors. Merchants displayed foreign goods and stocked up with new cargoes to take to their next port. Some traders sold slaves and the poor offered themselves for hire as laborers. Citizens met friends under the shady colonnades to discuss business deals, politics and new ideas. Women came to fill their water pots. Altars and statues honoring gods, local athletes and politicians were erected in many marketplaces. The center of Athens, surrounded by important government buildings, impressed all who visited the city.

LEAD WEIGHTS
Many things were sold by weight. In Athens, officials were chosen every year to inspect shopkeepers' weights. They checked that customers were not being cheated.

DID YOU KNOW?
Sparta did not issue coins until three centuries after the other city-states. The Spartans used iron rods for money until the fourth century BC.

TEXTILE TRADE
The Athenians on this pot are hurrying across the agora with bolts of cloth. Shops sold textiles made in foreign lands.

GOODS AND SERVICES
The marketplace provided all kinds of goods and services. Fishmongers sold fish, kept cool on marble slabs. Cobblers made sandals to fit the wearer's feet. Barbers trimmed hair and beards.

CENTRAL SPACE
In the agora at Athens, the city council met in one large building. Another big building housed public records and state documents. Merchants traded from stalls in the open square or from shops in the long, colonnaded buildings.

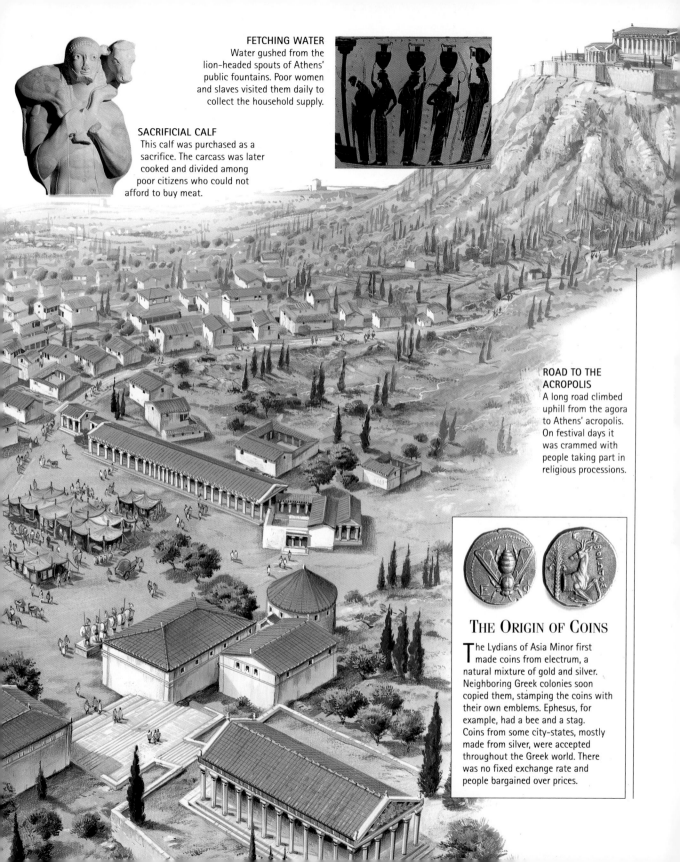

FETCHING WATER
Water gushed from the lion-headed spouts of Athens' public fountains. Poor women and slaves visited them daily to collect the household supply.

SACRIFICIAL CALF
This calf was purchased as a sacrifice. The carcass was later cooked and divided among poor citizens who could not afford to buy meat.

ROAD TO THE ACROPOLIS
A long road climbed uphill from the agora to Athens' acropolis. On festival days it was crammed with people taking part in religious processions.

THE ORIGIN OF COINS

The Lydians of Asia Minor first made coins from electrum, a natural mixture of gold and silver. Neighboring Greek colonies soon copied them, stamping the coins with their own emblems. Ephesus, for example, had a bee and a stag. Coins from some city-states, mostly made from silver, were accepted throughout the Greek world. There was no fixed exchange rate and people bargained over prices.

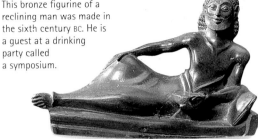

AT HIS EASE
This bronze figurine of a reclining man was made in the sixth century BC. He is a guest at a drinking party called a symposium.

A GOOD CATCH
Wall paintings at Akrotiri on the island of Thera tell us about Bronze Age life. Greeks have always depended on food from the sea.

• LIVING IN ANCIENT GREECE •

Eating and Drinking

In early times, the Greeks worked extremely hard to produce enough food. They did not always succeed, and there were famines during the Dark Age. Grape vines grew well on terraced hillsides and olive trees thrived in poor soil. But there was always the problem of needing more flat, fertile land for wheat and barley. Things improved once grain could be imported from the colonies or from Egypt. People ate greens—cabbage, lettuce, spinach and dandelion leaves—and root vegetables such as radishes, carrots and onions. Eggs, goat's milk cheese, almonds, figs and other fruit were also available. Squid, sea urchins, fish and shellfish were plentiful and provided protein. Meat was a rare treat reserved for the rich who could afford roast goat, sheep or pig, and for those who hunted wild deer, hares and boars. The Greeks sweetened their cakes and pastries with honey. Seasonings included garlic and herbs such as mint and marjoram.

STRINGED INSTRUMENTS
The kithara was a complicated form of lyre, usually played by professional musicians. They plucked the strings with a small instrument called a plectrum.

FEMALE COMPANIONS
Foreign or low-born women, called hetairai, amused the guests at symposiums. They were unmarried, beautiful, clever and trained in the art of conversation, making music and dancing.

MEN ONLY
Well-to-do Greek women did not attend symposiums, not even in their own homes. Slaves served the food and wine. Acrobats, jugglers and other professional performers provided entertainment.

DID YOU KNOW?

Greeks today use some vegetables that were unknown in ancient times. Peppers (capsicums), eggplants (aubergines), potatoes and tomatoes reached Europe in the 1500s, after the Spanish invasion of the Americas.

PARTY FOOD

At first, the food at symposiums was simple. By the third century BC, fashionable dinners began with roasted songbirds, artichoke hearts, mushrooms, grasshoppers, snails, fish roe and other snacks. Tuna fish, stuffed with herbs, might follow. Cooks often flavored the meat course with cheese and aniseed, and the feast finished with honeyed sweetmeats, nuts and seeds. Bread was part of every meal. The Greeks used olive oil instead of butter.

Discover more in End of an Empire

111

THE OLYMPIC OATH

During the Olympic ceremonies, a wild boar was sacrificed to Zeus. Athletes swore on this beast that they were freeborn Greeks and would not cheat.

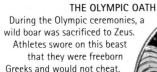

TEST OF STRENGTH

The winner in upright wrestling had to throw an opponent three times and push the back of his shoulders to the ground.

WOMEN'S GAMES

Women had their own games every four years to honor Hera, wife of Zeus. They ran foot races, which were divided into three different age groups.

• LIVING IN ANCIENT GREECE •

Festival Games

FIRST PRIZE

Winners at the Panathenaic Games in Athens received jars of olive oil. The jar was decorated with a scene from the winner's sport.

DRESSED IN OIL

Athletes competed naked in all events except the chariot race. They oiled their body thoroughly beforehand and afterwards cleaned their skin with bronze scrapers.

People believed that when the gods were happy they sent good fortune. They arranged festivals of music, poetry, drama and athletic games to please the gods. The four main festivals were the Olympic, the Pythian, the Isthmian and the Nemean. The five-day Olympic Games, honoring Zeus, took place in August every four years from 776 BC to AD 393. Wars between city-states ceased for a month beforehand so that thousands of priests, competitors and spectators from all over Greece could travel to Olympia in peace. The valley looked like a huge fairground. The visitors put up tents and there were food stalls and entertainers. Women did not compete in the games, but unmarried women, foreigners and slaves could watch from the stadium. Ancient Olympic events included running, wrestling, boxing, and chariot and horse races. Jockeys rode bareback, and horses frequently finished without their riders!

OLYMPIC CONTESTS
The pentathlon tested all-round athletes in five skills. These were running, long jumping, wrestling, javelin throwing and discus throwing. The discus was a heavy circular plate of stone or bronze. The athlete rubbed it with sand for a good grip.

CROWNING THE WINNER

Athletes trained hard for the games. Winners received woolen ribbons, jars of olive oil, palm branches and wreaths. The crowning wreaths were made from olive leaves at the Olympics, laurel leaves at the Pythian Games, pine needles at the Isthmian Games and parsley sprigs at the Nemean Games. Crowds went wild when successful athletes returned home. Some city-states gave them presents and great banquets. Statues of sporting superstars (above) stood beside those of the gods in the temples and open spaces at Olympia.

Discover more in City-states

113

Sickness and Health

The ancient Greeks admired physical fitness. Citizens gathered at the public "gymnasium" to practice sports, bathe and discuss philosophy. Studies of skeletons show that many women died at about 35 years of age and men at about 44. According to written records, some philosophers lived very long lives. For centuries, ancient Greeks believed that the gods sent accidents and illnesses as punishments. Asclepius, the god of healing (above left), usually carried a snake coiled around his staff. Sick people made sacrifices at his temples, then stayed overnight, hoping to be cured as they slept. The temple priests were Greece's first doctors. They treated their patients with a mixture of magic and herbs, special diets, rest or exercise. Towards the end of the fifth century BC, Greek physicians, led by Hippocrates, began to develop more successful methods of healing. They tried to find out how the body worked and what caused diseases. They also noted the effects of different medicines.

JASON THE PHYSICIAN
A man's tombstone often showed what he did for a living. Here, an Athenian doctor called Jason examines a boy with a very swollen belly.

DOCTOR'S APPOINTMENT
From the time of Hippocrates onward, blood was thought to contain disease. Doctors sometimes removed a little from a patient's arm. Physicians prescribed herbal remedies for many complaints and consulted scrolls of recorded medical information.

Eyebright
The ancient Greeks soaked eyebright in hot water to make an eyewash.

Hyssop
Hippocrates prescribed hyssop for coughs, bronchitis and other chest infections.

Mullein
Mullein, also an ancient treatment for coughs, is still used today.

Motherwort
Motherwort was thought to ease the pain of heart disease and childbirth.

Smooth sow thistle
This oddly named herb was supposed to relieve stomach complaints and scorpion bites.

THE FATHER OF MEDICINE

Hippocrates, the founder of scientific medicine, practiced and taught on the island of Cos. He said doctors could not understand the parts of the body until they understood the whole system. Hippocrates carefully observed patients' symptoms before making a diagnosis. In many countries, newly qualified doctors swear the Hippocratic oath, promising to care for the sick as well as they can.

SURGICAL INSTRUMENTS
Greek doctors did not perform many operations. Surgery, without anaesthetics and with simple instruments (right), was very painful. Patients often died from shock or infection.

DID YOU KNOW?
The ancient world had no protection against epidemic diseases. Between 430 and 429 BC, a terrible plague swept through Athens. The great Pericles was one of its victims.

WINE JUG
Some inventive potters began modeling parts of clay vessels. This jug, in the shape of a head, was made in the fourth century BC.

GIFTS FOR THE GODS
Small bronze horses, such as this mare with her foal, were made during the Geometric period. Worshippers left these statues in temples for the gods.

SHAPED IN TERRA-COTTA
Many Greek cities produced terra-cotta figurines, each developing its own style. This sphinx, dating from the late fifth to early fourth century BC, came from southern Italy.

• ARTS AND SCIENCE •

Clay and Metal

The ancient Greeks loved beauty. They wanted buildings and useful objects to be balanced and graceful. Designers calculated how to fill spaces with the perfect amount of decoration. Early potters fashioned elegant vessels to be used as drinking cups, water jugs, storage jars for wine and olive oil and for other practical purposes. From then onward, most potters used the same shapes. Large numbers of craftworkers made sandals, furniture, cooking vessels and other items for everyday use.

In Athens, workshops lining the agora's south and west sides produced pottery, bronze and marble goods, and terra-cotta figurines. Athenian potters also lived and worked beside the cemetery. Metalworkers had quarters near the temple of Hephaestus—their special god. They used bronze for armor and household articles, and harder iron for tools and weapons that required sharp edges. Coins and jewelry were often made from gold and silver. Many craftworkers, especially those who produced weapons and armor, became very rich.

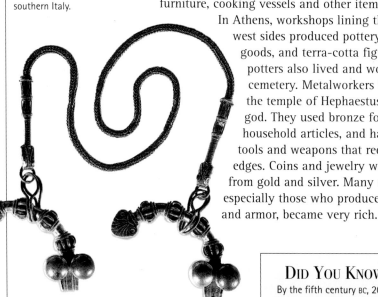

SILVER CHAIN
As the centuries passed, jewelers became more skilled at working silver and gold. This silver necklace was probably made in northern Greece between 420 and 400 BC.

DID YOU KNOW?
By the fifth century BC, 20,000 slaves were laboring in the silver mines near Athens. They worked shifts of ten hours in narrow tunnels lit by oil lamps.

POTTERY WORKSHOP
The use of the wheel gave potters both hands free to shape the clay. They prepared slip, a special liquid clay, for decoration and then fired the vessels in a kiln. Sometimes touches of color were added to the pots after firing.

THE BLACK AND THE RED

Thousands of pots survive from all over ancient Greece. From about 550 to 300 BC, Athenian "figure" ware was more popular than any other pottery. The vessels showed scenes from the lives of gods and heroes, as well as everyday subjects. Vase painters first developed the black-figure technique—drawing black figures on a red clay background (below left). Later, the red-figure technique (below right) became fashionable. Painters covered the red clay surface with a black slip background and left the figures outlined in red.

RUINS AT CORINTH
The temple of Apollo at Corinth was built of limestone in about 540 BC. At the time it was coated in white plaster to look like marble.

Building in Stone

F ew houses or early public buildings of ancient Greece survive. They were made of timber and sun-dried mud bricks, and have crumbled and rotted away. Later structures of marble and limestone have survived earthquakes, fires, wars and weather. Throughout the Greek world, priests and priestesses cared for sacred sites. The best known site was the Acropolis, the hill overlooking Athens, where there was a collection of temples, altars, statues and memorial stones, as well as the state treasury. The Parthenon, a temple decorated with enormous sculptures, housed a statue of Athena. Pheidias, the sculptor in charge, made it from wood, gold and ivory. Like many other temples, the Parthenon was huge, rectangular in shape and surrounded by grooved (fluted) columns. The pieces of each column were heaved into place with winches and pulleys. Architects used clever tricks in their buildings such as making columns lean slightly inwards so that they would appear straight up and down from a distance.

PARTHENON RUINS
The Parthenon was built in Doric style between 447 and 432 BC. Plastic copies of the original marble-relief friezes are being used to restore the building.

HORSEMEN IN PROCESSION
A marble-relief frieze almost 525 ft (160 m) long ran like a ribbon under the roof around the Parthenon's four outer walls. It showed the Panathenaic festival procession.

PORCH OF THE MAIDENS
Statues of young women, called caryatids, were used to support the roof. The Erechtheum's caryatids are the most famous in Greece.

THREE GREEK ORDERS
The Greeks built in three styles called orders. The plainer Doric order (left) came first and was always the favorite. The Corinthian (right) developed from the Ionic (center).

THE ROMAN ORDERS

The Romans built many temples and public buildings in the style of the Greeks. They copied the Doric, Ionic and Corinthian orders, and developed two more orders of their own—Tuscan and Composite. The Tuscan order was very plain, without fluting on the columns or ornamental moldings. The richly decorated Composite order combined features of the Ionic and the Corinthian.

Tuscan

Composite

THE ERECHTHEUM
The Erechtheum, a temple on the Acropolis, protected an old wooden statue of Athena. It was built in Ionic style on two levels and had several porches.

119

Going to War

The ancient Greek city-states fought each other over land and trade. Sparta had a full-time army, but other city-states trained freeborn men to fight and called them up in times of war. In Athens, men aged between 20 and 50 had to defend their state whenever necessary. Greeks who could afford horses usually joined the cavalry, but most served as foot soldiers called hoplites. Poorer citizens who were unable to buy their own weapons and armor rowed the warships. When the Persians invaded Greece, some city-states banded together against the foreigners. The Persian Wars lasted from 490 to 449 BC, and in 480 BC the Persian army destroyed Athens. In 447 BC the Greeks rebuilt the city. Sparta fought Athens for 27 years in the Peloponnesian War from 431 to 404 BC. Both sides were supported by other city-states. Sparta eventually won, but every city-state that took part in the conflict was weakened by loss of lives and money.

BATTLE SCENES
War was a common theme in vase art. These paintings provide useful information about the way warriors dressed for battle and the weapons they used.

DID YOU KNOW?
The Athenian navy had long, narrow, timber warships called triremes. In battle, a trireme was powered by 170 oarsmen. They tried to sink enemy ships by ramming them with the bronze prow.

BODY SHIELDS

Hoplites carried shields, made of bronze or leather, to protect them from neck to thigh. The symbols on the soldiers' shields represented their family or city.

FIGHTING THE AMAZONS

The Amazons were legendary women warriors who were believed to have helped Troy in the Trojan War. This marble frieze shows the Greeks and Amazons fighting.

PROTECTIVE CLOTHING

Soldiers wore bronze or leather breast and back plates joined on the shoulders and at the sides. Helmets, which came in various styles, protected their head and face.

VICTORY AT SEA

After the Persians destroyed Athens, the Greek fleet trapped the Persian fleet in a narrow channel of water between the island of Salamis and the Greek mainland. There, the Greek triremes rammed the larger Persian warships and forced them to retreat.

FIRST HISTORIANS

Herodotus, who wrote a history of the Persian Wars, has been called the father of history. He traveled widely to get information for his books. Another ancient Greek called Thucydides wrote a history of the Peloponnesian War. Both Herodotus and Thucydides tried to write factual accounts of what had happened. They interviewed many people who had fought in the wars.

Q: What did a Greek hoplite wear to battle?

COURAGEOUS LEADER
Alexander the Great was a fearless soldier and was often wounded. This mosaic shows him riding, without a helmet, into the thick of the Battle of Issus against King Darius of Persia.

MACEDONIAN MEDALLIONS
These medallions were found in Egypt. The one on the left shows Philip II with his attendants. The other portrays Alexander.

• FOREIGN AFFAIRS •

The Macedonians

Macedonia in northeastern Greece was not a democratic city-state. It was ruled by kings who claimed to be descended from Macedon, a son of Zeus. For centuries, Macedonia was weak and frequently overrun by invaders. When Philip II came to power, he began to improve Macedonia's fortunes. By 338 BC, he controlled all of Greece and afterwards declared war on Persia. When Philip II was murdered in 336 BC, he was succeeded by his 20-year-old son Alexander, who eventually conquered Persia in 333 BC. Alexander (left) had blond hair and eyes of different colors—gray-blue and dark brown. He loved reading the *Iliad* and modeled himself on two great heroes, Achilles and Heracles. Alexander fought many successful battles and seized kingdoms throughout the eastern world. He earned the title "the Great" and married a Persian princess. When he died in 323 BC, his vast empire stretched as far as India.

HUNTING FOR SPORT
Alexander, whether hunting or fighting, was a popular subject with sculptors. This is part of a carving on the tomb of a king of Sidon in ancient Phoenicia.

ON THE MOVE
The Macedonian army trudged long distances through deserts and over mountains. Besides thousands of cavalry and foot soldiers, there were servants, grooms, women, children, pack animals and wagons. Indian elephants became part of the Macedonian army after Alexander's death.

FIGHTING IN FORMATION

Philip II trained his hoplites to fight in a formation called a phalanx. In battle, the front ranks extended their long spears. The men behind rested their spears on the row in front to form a barrier against arrows. A phalanx's weakest point was the right side, where the men were only half protected by their shields. Flute music helped the marching hoplites to stay in step.

DID YOU KNOW?

When Alexander was eight or nine, he tamed a pedigree stallion that had defeated his father's horse trainers. Alexander rode this horse, Bucephalus, into almost all his major battles.

ROMAN IMITATION
Roman sculptors copied the best Greek statues, especially those from the Hellenistic era. This is a Roman statue of the goddess Aphrodite, known to the Romans as Venus.

The Hellenistic World

The ancient Greeks called their country "Hellas" and themselves "Hellenes." After Alexander the Great died, the three generals Antigonus, Seleucus and Ptolemy divided up his empire between them. Antigonus ruled Macedonia and the rest of Greece and founded the Antigonid royal family. Seleucus took Asia Minor, Persia, and other eastern countries and began the Seleucid line of rulers. Ptolemy governed Egypt as the first ruler of the Ptolemaic dynasty. This was the beginning of the Hellenistic Age when Greek customs and ideas spread far beyond the boundaries of Greece. Architects building new cities throughout the Hellenistic world used Greek styles. These settlements adopted Greek law and language and the people attended Greek entertainment in theaters and stadiums. Hellenistic artists were interested in realism. Portraits on coins throughout the empire began to represent people's faces rather than making everyone look like gods or heroes. Sculptors chose a wider range of subjects and showed childhood, old age and suffering in a realistic way.

LIFELIKE IN STONE
Hellenistic sculptures showed movement and feeling. This Altar of Zeus at Pergamum in modern Turkey features warring gods and giants.

THE PTOLEMIES OF EGYPT

The Ptolemy dynasty governed Egypt from 323 to 30 BC. In Alexandria, Ptolemy I (left) built a huge library that had laboratories, observatories and a zoo. This city soon became the most important center of learning in the ancient world. The Ptolemy dynasty taught the Egyptians many Greek ways, but Cleopatra VII, the last ruler of the dynasty, was the only one who spoke Egyptian as well as Greek. After her death, the Romans took over Egypt.

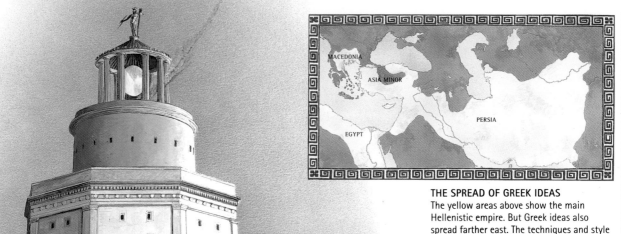

THE SPREAD OF GREEK IDEAS
The yellow areas above show the main Hellenistic empire. But Greek ideas also spread farther east. The techniques and style of Hellenistic art influenced ancient religious sculptures in Pakistan and Afghanistan.

THE FACE OF MEDUSA
This Hellenistic statue of Medusa, one of the hideous Gorgons, adorns a temple in Turkey. Her features, especially the dimpled chin, are more human-looking than earlier statues. Ringlets replace the snaky hair.

ALEXANDRIA
Alexander the Great set up many new cities called Alexandria. The first one, where he was later buried, was in Egypt. A three-tiered lighthouse was built in the harbor. The light from the fire at the base was reflected by a series of bronze mirrors and could be seen far out at sea.

TWO NAMES—ONE GOD
The Romans renamed most of the Greek gods and heroes when they adopted Greek mythology as their own. Hephaestus, the Greek god of fire, became Vulcan.

VULCAN. [1032] K

• FOREIGN AFFAIRS •

End of an Empire

The division of Alexander the Great's empire by his generals weakened Greece's hold on the ancient world. From 509 BC, a new power—Rome—had been growing in Italy. Roman rule spread gradually across the Hellenistic world. In 275 BC, the Romans captured the Greek colonies in southern Italy and Sicily. Between 148 and 146 BC, Macedonia and all of southern Greece became part of the Roman Empire. To the east, the Hellenistic empire slipped away as Rome acquired one kingdom after another. Finally, the Roman emperor Augustus defeated the Egyptians in 31 BC and demanded Cleopatra VII's surrender. The following year Cleopatra killed herself and Egypt became the last province in the Greek empire to fall into Roman hands. Although Greece no longer existed as a political and military power, Greek literature, art and architecture became models for the Romans who also adopted Greek gods and heroes. Many Roman boys were educated in Athens before Athenian schools closed down in the sixth century AD.

GODDESS JUNO
This Roman bust of Juno, wife of Jupiter, was copied from a Greek original. In Greek mythology, Juno and Jupiter were known as Hera and Zeus.

TRAVELING TREASURES

The Romans admired and valued Greek sculpture and other works of art. They stole many treasures on their journey of conquest through the Greek city-states. Roman generals organized triumphant processions to carry the treasures through the streets of Rome.

THE GREEK ORTHODOX CHURCH

Byzantium was a Greek colony from mid-600 BC until the Romans occupied it in mid-100 BC. The Roman emperor Constantine renamed the city Constantinople. This city became the center of eastern Christendom and Christians living there founded the Greek Orthodox Church. Religious pictures, called icons (above), are sacred to Greek Orthodox worshippers. Early religious artists used ancient Greek styles. Constantinople is now Istanbul, the capital of Turkey.

TEMPLE OF ZEUS

The Roman architect Cossutius began the temple of Zeus in Athens in 174 BC. This Corinthian-style building, which took until AD 132 to finish, was the largest Hellenistic shrine on mainland Greece.

PORTRAIT ON WOOD

Like the Egyptians, Roman citizens living in Egypt mummified their dead. Roman artists copied Greek styles and painted lifelike portraits, such as this, on the mummy cases

Discover more in Writing and Education

Ancient Rome

- Why did people go to the forum?

- Which Roman god had two faces?

- Why did the emperor Hadrian have a wall built in Britain?

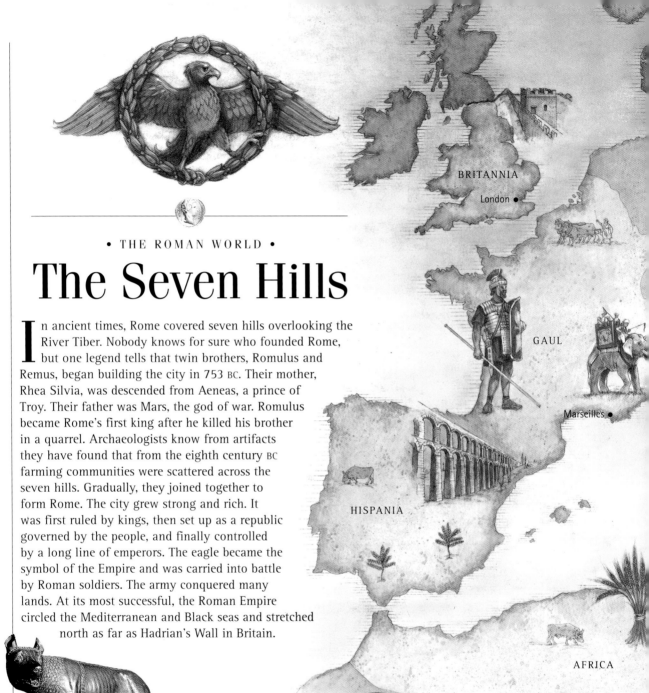

• THE ROMAN WORLD •
The Seven Hills

In ancient times, Rome covered seven hills overlooking the River Tiber. Nobody knows for sure who founded Rome, but one legend tells that twin brothers, Romulus and Remus, began building the city in 753 BC. Their mother, Rhea Silvia, was descended from Aeneas, a prince of Troy. Their father was Mars, the god of war. Romulus became Rome's first king after he killed his brother in a quarrel. Archaeologists know from artifacts they have found that from the eighth century BC farming communities were scattered across the seven hills. Gradually, they joined together to form Rome. The city grew strong and rich. It was first ruled by kings, then set up as a republic governed by the people, and finally controlled by a long line of emperors. The eagle became the symbol of the Empire and was carried into battle by Roman soldiers. The army conquered many lands. At its most successful, the Roman Empire circled the Mediterranean and Black seas and stretched north as far as Hadrian's Wall in Britain.

BRITANNIA

London •

GAUL

Marseilles •

HISPANIA

AFRICA

ROMAN LEGEND
Rhea Silvia's jealous uncle ordered that Romulus and Remus should be drowned in the River Tiber. A she-wolf discovered the babies and fed them with her milk.

THE PORT OF ROME
Ostia, at the mouth of the River Tiber, is about 16 miles (25 km) by road from the city of Rome. This coin shows ships in Ostia's ancient harbor.

753 BC
The legendary date for the founding of Rome.

753–510 BC
Rome is ruled by a series of kings.

510–27 BC
The Roman Republic.

27 BC
The Roman Empire is established under Augustus, the first emperor,

AD 395
The Empire is split into West and East.

AD 476
The Western Empire collapses.

AD 1453
The last city of the Eastern (Byzantine) Roman Empire is captured.

GERMANIA

DACIA

BLACK SEA

Ravenna

MACEDONIA

Constantinople

ADRIATIC SEA

ASIA

RSICA

Rome
Ostia

Pompeii

ACHAEA

SYRIA

CYPRUS

Athens

ARDINIA

AEGEAN SEA

Damascus

IONIAN SEA

SICILIA

CRETA

Jerusalem

MEDITERRANEAN SEA

JUDAEA

Carthage

Alexandria

AEGYPTUS

DID YOU KNOW?

"Italos" was the Greek word for bull-calf. Because the earliest Romans used cattle as a form of money, this "land of calves" soon became known as Italy.

Discover more in Empire in Decline

131

MYTHICAL BEAST
The Etruscans adopted some figures from Greek mythology, such as this lion-like monster called a chimaera. It has a goat's head in the middle of its back and a serpent for a tail.

BANQUETING IN STYLE
Large wall paintings in Etruscan tombs, which were sealed off from the air for about 2,500 years, have lasted amazingly well. Scenes, such as this one of people at a sumptuous banquet, show how much the Etruscans enjoyed themselves.

• THE ROMAN WORLD •

The Etruscans

People lived in Italy long before Rome was built. There were Latins, Samnites, Umbrians, Sabines, Greeks and the most powerful of all—the Etruscans. They occupied Etruria, which spread to the north and south of Rome. Etruria had a good climate, rich soil for farming, rocks containing useful metal ores, and thick forests to provide wood for building houses, temples, boats and bridges. One story suggests that the Etruscans came to Italy from Lydia in Asia Minor when food was scarce in their own country. Archaeologists cannot prove this, but they know a great deal about Etruscan daily life and their well-planned cities from what these early settlers buried in their tombs. They furnished the underground tombs like their homes with many fine bronze and terracotta clay statues. The Etruscans excelled at making music, and raising and riding horses. They were also skilled engineers. At times Etruscan kings ruled Rome, and the Etruscans and Latins later became one group of people.

GUARDIAN OF THE GATE
This two-faced god is looking forwards and backwards in time. He may be an earlier Etruscan version of Janus, the Roman god of exits and entrances.

MODELED IN TERRA-COTTA
In the ancient world, men and women usually dined separately. In Etruria, however, husbands and wives often feasted together, as shown on the lid of this coffin.

ON GUARD
Etruscan sculptors made many statues from bronze. They often portrayed warriors with huge, crested helmets, which made the soldiers look taller and thinner.

TELLING THE FUTURE

The Etruscans worshiped many gods. Priests, called augurs, claimed they could tell what the gods wanted from certain natural signs. They read meaning into thunder, lightning, and the flight of birds, and told the future from the insides of dead animals, especially the liver. This replica of a sheep's liver (left) is marked out in sections, each with the name of a different god. It was possibly used by augurs when examining a liver, as shown on the back of the mirror above.

Government

Kings ruled Rome until 510 BC when the citizens expelled the last king, Tarquin the Proud. Rome then became a republic governed by officials who were elected by the people. Each year, the citizens chose two consuls and other government administrators from a group called the Senate. The idea was to prevent any one man from having too much power. Julius Caesar (above left), a brilliant general, had many military successes, which helped him to gain popularity and power in the Republic. In 49 BC, he marched his army to Rome and seized power. A civil war followed in which Caesar defeated his rivals and became the ruler of Rome. This one-man rule worried some senators and Caesar was murdered in 44 BC. His death brought renewed civil war and the collapse of the Republic. Caesar's adopted son Octavian gained control and brought peace to the Roman world. Octavian was renamed Augustus, and in 27 BC he became the first of Rome's many emperors. Some emperors, such as Augustus and Trajan, governed well. Others, such as Domitian and Nero, used their power badly.

CITY CENTER
The heart of every Roman town and city was the forum. This open square was surrounded by government buildings and temples. People came to the forum to vote, hear speeches, attend the law courts, read public notices and discuss the issues of the day.

DID YOU KNOW?
Roman emperors did not wear crowns like kings. Instead, they wore laurel wreaths on their heads. These had once been given to generals to celebrate victories in battle.

SYMBOL OF LAW
The fasces was a bundle of rods and an axe that symbolized the power of a magistrate. It was carried for him by his young attendant. The Romans took this symbol from the Etruscans.

HONORING AUGUSTUS
The marble Altar of Augustan Peace in Rome is carved on all sides with subjects that reflect the greatness of Rome's first emperor, Augustus. This panel shows members of the imperial family.

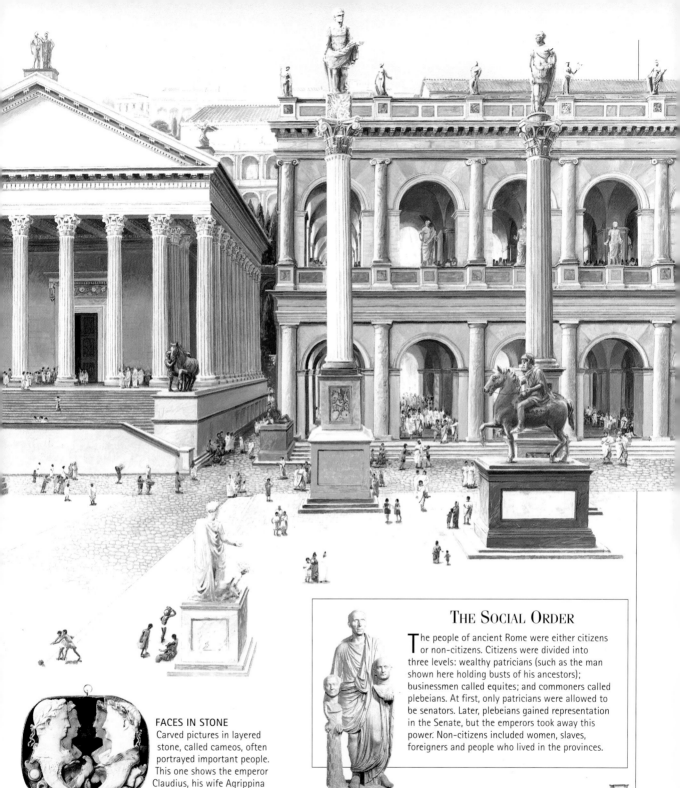

FACES IN STONE
Carved pictures in layered stone, called cameos, often portrayed important people. This one shows the emperor Claudius, his wife Agrippina the Younger, and her relatives.

THE SOCIAL ORDER

The people of ancient Rome were either citizens or non-citizens. Citizens were divided into three levels: wealthy patricians (such as the man shown here holding busts of his ancestors); businessmen called equites; and commoners called plebeians. At first, only patricians were allowed to be senators. Later, plebeians gained representation in the Senate, but the emperors took away this power. Non-citizens included women, slaves, foreigners and people who lived in the provinces.

Discover more in Growing Empire

Worshiping the Gods

RELIGION FROM EGYPT
The worship of Isis, the goddess of heaven and earth, first became fashionable in Rome after the Egyptian Queen Cleopatra spent a year there. Later, Isis had followers throughout the Empire.

The ancient Romans worshiped the same gods as the Greeks, but they gave them different names. The Greek god Zeus, for example, was called Jupiter, and the goddess Hera became Juno. People worshiped their gods through prayer, offerings of food and wine, and animal sacrifices. They also believed that natural things, such as trees and rivers, and objects that were made, such as doors, hinges and doorsteps, all had their own divine spirits. The head of the household was responsible for religious rituals in the home. Government officials performed religious duties in temples. Priests, called augurs, examined the insides of dead animals and looked for meaning in the flight of birds, which they believed were messengers from the gods. The expansion of the Empire introduced the Romans to new religions. These were permitted, provided worshipers did not ignore the Roman gods or threaten Roman government. The Jews and the Christians endured centuries of hardship because their beliefs challenged the emperors' authority.

HOUSEHOLD SHRINE
Every Roman house had an altar for the household gods. Here, spirits of the home, the larder and the family's special god (center) stand above a sacred serpent.

WORSHIPING BACCHUS
Followers of Dionysus sacrificed goats to him. This Greek god of wine and the theater was known to the ancient Romans as Bacchus (right).

A PERSIAN GOD
Many Roman soldiers worshipped Mithras, the bull-slayer, god of light and wisdom. Mithras was supposed to have been born holding a sword.

A TEMPLE FOR AUGUSTUS
This temple at Nîmes, in what is now France, was built during the reign of the emperor Augustus. It was dedicated to the worship of the emperor.

THE VESTAL VIRGINS

Vesta, the goddess of the hearth, was worshiped in every household. Six priestesses, called Vestal Virgins, tended her state shrine in Rome's forum. They had to keep her sacred flame burning continuously. It was a great honor to be chosen as a Vestal Virgin.

THE GOD OF BEGINNINGS

Two-faced Janus, looking backwards and forwards, supposedly understood both the past and the future. Janus was the god of beginnings—such as the first hour of the day. The first month of the year, January, was named after him. This early Roman god of exits and entrances guarded doors, gateways and arches. The doors to his shrine in Rome were always open in times of war, but closed during peace.

JOINING OF HANDS
A Roman bride wore a white tunic, a saffron-colored veil and a wreath made from marjoram. The couple clasped right hands while the marriage contract was read and sealed. Later, the groom carried the bride over the threshold of her new home.

FACES FROM THE PAST
Roman couples often had their likenesses painted on wood or as frescoes on the walls of their houses. This portrait was found in a house at Pompeii.

AT PLAY
Rich women amused themselves by playing music. They often sat on high-backed bronze chairs, which were a sign of wealth. Most Romans sat on wooden stools.

• LIVING IN THE EMPIRE •

Marriage and Home Life

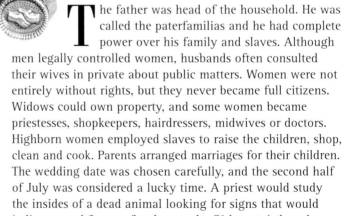

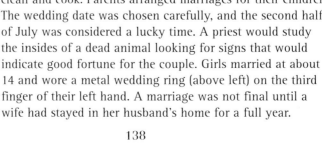

The father was head of the household. He was called the paterfamilias and he had complete power over his family and slaves. Although men legally controlled women, husbands often consulted their wives in private about public matters. Women were not entirely without rights, but they never became full citizens. Widows could own property, and some women became priestesses, shopkeepers, hairdressers, midwives or doctors. Highborn women employed slaves to raise the children, shop, clean and cook. Parents arranged marriages for their children. The wedding date was chosen carefully, and the second half of July was considered a lucky time. A priest would study the insides of a dead animal looking for signs that would indicate good fortune for the couple. Girls married at about 14 and wore a metal wedding ring (above left) on the third finger of their left hand. A marriage was not final until a wife had stayed in her husband's home for a full year.

138

TIME TO CELEBRATE
This children's procession was held in Ostia. Processions were a way of celebrating religious festivals, battle victories and weddings.

WRITING ON WAX
This girl holds wooden tablets that are coated on one side with wax and tied together to form a type of notebook. She is writing with a bone stylus.

• LIVING IN THE EMPIRE •

Children and Education

W ealthy couples thought children were a blessing and hoped to have large families. But women often died in childbirth and many babies and small children did not survive because the Romans had little knowledge of hygiene and childhood diseases. Parents sometimes abandoned their sickly infants outside the city's walls. Poor people found children costly to raise and their offspring went to work at an early age without any schooling. There was no free education in ancient Rome, and when children were about six, those from wealthy families started school where fees had to be paid, or began lessons at home. Many families employed educated Greek slaves as tutors. At 11, some boys went to secondary schools where they learned history, geography, geometry, astronomy, music and philosophy. At 14, boys who wanted a career in politics or law began to study public speaking. Girls learned basic reading, writing and mathematics and how to run a home.

A BOY'S LIFE
This carving shows four stages in a boy's childhood: at his mother's breast, accepted by his father, riding in a toy chariot drawn by a donkey, and with his teacher.

A NEW BABY
A father held his newborn infant in his arms to show that he accepted his son or daughter. In a ceremony nine days after being born, the baby received a name and a neck charm, called a bulla, to ward off evil spirits.

LEARNING LESSONS

Schoolboys read their lessons from long papyrus scrolls. Papyrus came from Egypt where the plants grew plentifully beside the River Nile. Paper was made by beating the fibers of the stems.

THE TOGA OF MANHOOD

At the age of 14, boys were expected to behave as men. Every March, during the feast of the god Bacchus, special coming-of-age ceremonies for citizens' sons were held in the forum. The boys took off their neck charms (right), and exchanged their childhood clothing for adult togas. Barbers gave them their first shave and they were registered as citizens. The ceremonies ended with the boys making offerings of sacred honey cakes on the altar of Bacchus.

MOTHER AND CHILD

This gravestone in Palmyra, Syria is an early tribute to a mother and child. The theme is repeated in Christian paintings of Mary and Jesus.

SPRING BOUQUET
Here, Primavera, the goddess of spring, walks through the countryside gathering flowers. Her clothing, falling in soft folds, shows the elegance of fashionable female dress.

DRESSED FOR BEST
Fashions in clothing were slow to change in ancient Roman times. These two people are dressed in early Empire style. The woman is wearing a short tunic under a full-length one and has a long robe draped over the top. The man is clad in tunic and toga.

• LIVING IN THE EMPIRE •

Togas and Tunics

Togas, the dress of citizens, were first worn by the Etruscans. Although togas were uncomfortable and difficult to keep clean, these garments were popular with the emperors and remained fashionable for centuries. They were semicircular in shape and usually made from a single length of woolen cloth. The wearer held the heavy folds together as he moved, which left only the right arm free. Emperors wore purple togas; senators' togas were white and edged with a purple stripe. Citizens wore wool or linen tunics under their plain white togas, but other men, women and children wore tunics only. These were folded and pinned, and held with a belt. They seldom had stitched seams because sewing with thick bone or bronze needles was so difficult. During imperial times, wealthy people liked clothing made from finely woven Indian cotton and expensive Chinese silk. Jewelers crafted beautiful ornaments, such as gold earrings (above left). Women also wore jewelry made of polished amber from the cold Baltic countries, which was carved in the town of Aquileia in northeast Italy.

142

DELICATE JEWELRY
Jewelers worked with many precious stones and metals imported from the provinces. This necklace is made from emeralds threaded on gold rods and joined with gold links.

IN FASHION
Beards went in and out of fashion through the centuries. In the second century AD, emperors such as Hadrian and Septimius Severus (right) led a trend towards beards.

SWEET PERFUMES
Women used great quantities of sweet-smelling oils. The most expensive came from Arabia and were bought in glass bottles, such as this one, from shops that specialized in perfumes and scented ointments.

HAIRSTYLES OF THE EMPIRE

Slaves spent hours dressing their mistresses' hair. They dyed and perfumed it, curled it with heated tongs, and coiled it into buns. Slaves who did a bad job could be beaten. Sometimes, dark-haired Roman ladies wore wigs made from blonde locks, or had hairpieces fixed in place with hairpins. Hairstyles changed often. Vibia Matidia, the emperor Trajan's niece (far right), and Faustina (right), wife of the emperor Marcus Aurelius, have two different imperial hairstyles.

Discover more in Food and Feasts

SEWER SYSTEMS
Sewers carried running water to private lavatories in wealthy homes and to public lavatories in the streets. In Rome, the waste ran into the River Tiber.

City Life

Roman cities were laid out in a square with the main roads crossing at right angles. Buildings included a basilica that contained offices and law courts, temples, shops, workshops, public bathhouses and public lavatories. Aqueducts brought in water, while sewers removed waste. There was often a theater for plays and an amphitheater for other entertainments. Statues and decorated arches and columns were erected to commemorate important events. Cities were crowded and dirty. The rich had spacious town houses but most people lived in cramped conditions. Blocks of flats made of stone and wood were three to five storeys high. Sometimes they collapsed because they were so badly built. Most houses had no plumbing, and residents tipped waste down communal drains. Later, when the city of Rome became extremely overcrowded, the emperor passed a law forbidding people to move wheeled vehicles in daylight, so carts clattered after dark. The poet Martial complained, "there's nowhere a poor man can get any quiet in Rome."

CITY SHOPPING
There were no supermarkets in Rome. Small shops specialized in particular goods. These relief carvings show a greengrocer (top) and a butcher (bottom).

STREET SCENE
Rome's narrow side streets were lined with stalls and shops. At night, the shopkeepers secured their goods behind heavy wooden shutters. Walls were covered with signs and advertisements. Some people carried their wares while others used donkeys to transport their goods.

TAKE-OUT SHOP
Most apartments had no kitchens. Hot food was sold from shops (right) and stalls, and many people cooked in the street using portable stoves.

In Memoriam

Ancient Romans cremated or buried the dead, and believed that their spirits crossed the mythical River Styx to the Underworld (Hades). A coin placed in the dead person's mouth paid the ferryboat fare. Mourners and musicians accompanied the body through the streets to the cemetery outside the city's walls. Many monuments to the dead survive. The one above presents portraits of two freed slaves surrounded by the rods and staffs of the freedom ceremony (left), metalworker's tools (top) and carpenter's tools (right).

Did You Know?

City dwellers greatly feared fires. These were easily started by candles, oil lamps and portable stoves. Rome had seven fire brigades, equipped with hand pumps, buckets, hooks and axes, but they seldom managed to save houses that caught fire.

The emperor Hadrian's villa at Tibur (now called Tivoli), near Rome, was set in a beautifully landscaped garden. Greek sculptures stood beside the many lakes and waterways.

COUNTRY ART
People spent a great deal of money on their country villas. Wall paintings, such as this one, sculptures and mosaics were just as elaborate as the art that decorated town houses.

• LIVING IN THE EMPIRE •

Country Life

Throughout Italy and the provinces, large farming estates produced food for city dwellers and the army. Provinces such as Egypt and North Africa grew grain, Spain was famous for olive oil, Italy made the best wines, and Britain supplied beer and woolen goods. Farm slaves toiled from dawn to dusk, and were frequently whipped by the overseers who supervised them in the fields. Oxen and cattle pulled plows, and donkeys and mules were used for other work. The famous Roman poet Virgil wrote a practical handbook for farmers in the form of a poem called the *Georgics*. In it, he advised them to "enrich the dried-up soil with dung," and told them how to rotate crops and keep corn free of weeds. The crops grown depended largely on soil and climate. In Italy, farmers grew grapes, olives and many vegetables. Pork was a favorite meat, and large numbers of pigs were raised. Sheep and goats were kept for wool and milk. Farmers also raised chickens, ducks, geese and pigeons, and kept bees for their honey.

DID YOU KNOW?
In the fourth century AD, St. Augustine wrote about the number of spirit gods worshiped by country people. At least 12 gods were linked to the growing of crops. Silvanus, for example, was the spirit of the boundary between cultivated fields and woodland.

COUNTRY HOLIDAY
Wealthy Romans owned luxurious houses in the country. Set among the estate's plowed fields, orchards and livestock barns, the "villa urbana" had all the comforts of the owner's town dwelling. The part of the estate that housed the farm staff was called the "villa rustica."

GARDEN FRESCO
Livia, wife of the emperor Augustus, had a villa at Primaporta outside Rome. This fresco on the wall of one of the small rooms created a cool feeling during summer.

FARMING IN THE EMPIRE

By imperial times, much land had been organized into large estates and small farms were unusual. Wealthy landowners, living mostly in town, employed farm managers and slaves. Farming methods changed little over the centuries. Oxen pulled plows or pushed threshing machines. Farm workers wielded iron hoes, rakes, scythes and sickles, and stomped the juice from grapes. In later times, Roman engineers invented waterwheels to grind corn. These saved much time and energy.

MAKING MOSAICS
Mosaicists used hammers and chisels to cut sandstone and marble into small colored cubes called tesserae. Working over a pattern or picture, they pressed the tesserae and pieces of glass into a bedding of soft mortar. Finally, they cleaned and polished the surface thoroughly.

DID YOU KNOW?
Pottery was traded across the Empire. Scientists can now find out where the clay came from originally by examining tiny pieces under powerful microscopes, or by chemical analysis of fragments.

DANCING FAUN
This bronze faun, a country god, stood in the courtyard of a house in Pompeii. Like so many other Roman statues, it was copied from a Greek sculpture.

RESTING EMPRESS
A full-length marble statue was a common form of portrait for important people during imperial times. This is Agrippina, wife of the emperor Claudius.

• LIVING IN THE EMPIRE •
Craft Skills

In small workshops behind city shops, craftworkers turned metal, clay, stone, glass, wood, animal bones, ivory, cloth, leather and other materials into useful and decorative objects. Potteries in Gaul (present-day France), Italy and North Africa produced great numbers of red pots, which were exported all over the Empire. Fresco painters, stonemasons, mosaicists and carpenters worked at people's houses or on public buildings, which were often commissioned by the emperors. Cameo carving (the art of making pictures from layered stone) and mosaic (the art of making designs from small pieces of colored stone and glass) were both popular during the time of the Empire. Cameo carvers usually worked with sardonyx, a semiprecious stone that formed naturally in layers of different colors. In the centuries before the Empire, generations of Roman craftworkers learned from Etruscan art and from Greek pottery, painting and sculpture. They copied Greek statues and the technique of carving friezes in stone. Craftworkers passed on their skills to their sons.

CARVED GLASS
The dark inner layer of this glass vase was encased in opaque white glass, which was then skillfully cut away to produce the decoration.

DRINKING CUPS
Silver cups survive from the first century BC. This one features a scene from a Greek tragedy by Sophocles.

BLOWING GLASS
Glass-blowing, which was developed in the first century BC, was an important technological breakthrough. Glass-blowing probably began in Syria, but it spread quickly across the West. Glass workshops were hot and uncomfortable, but this new technique allowed skilled craftworkers to make objects in many shapes. Sometimes they combined old molding methods with blowing. Glass became a cheap, everyday material, and most people throughout the Empire could afford some glassware.

DRINKING DOVES
This mosaic, made from thousands of tesserae, decorated the emperor Hadrian's villa. The Roman artist copied a Greek original.

Discover more in The Etruscans

DAILY EXERCISE
Some young women exercised daily in the gymnasiums to keep trim. The ancient Romans believed that a healthy body ensured a healthy mind.

THE ORDER OF BATHING
Bathers began in a warm room with a pool filled with tepid water. Next, they moved to the steam room where the water was very hot. Finally, they plunged into cold water to cool off. Slaves attended to bathers' needs, cleaned the baths and stoked the furnaces.

• LIVING IN THE EMPIRE •

Staying Healthy

Diseases such as typhoid, dysentery and tuberculosis killed many people in the Empire's overcrowded cities, but minor ailments could also be serious. Cures were often unsuccessful because doctors did not understand the causes of illness. Treatments depended on basic scientific knowledge combined with folklore and prayer. The Empire's only hospitals were reserved for wounded soldiers. Every town had at least one public bathhouse, and cities often had several. Entrance fees were low for both men and women; children were admitted free. In Rome, besides baths, these huge complexes contained gymnasiums, massage rooms, take-out food shops, libraries, and gardens where citizens met to exchange gossip and news. The emperors Titus, Trajan, Caracalla and Diocletian all sponsored the building of public bathhouses. The Baths of Caracalla could take 1,600 bathers a day. Tooth decay was not a serious problem for ancient Romans because they had no sugar in their diet. Honey was expensive and used sparingly.

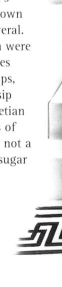

BODY OIL
This oil flask and tools, called strigils, once belonged to a Roman athlete. Athletes oiled their bodies before exercising and scraped themselves clean afterwards.

150

HEALING WATER
The baths at Bath in England are filled with water from natural hot springs. These were sacred to the ancient Romans and used for healing purposes.

MEDICAL MATTERS

Many doctors practicing in ancient Rome were Greek slaves or freedmen. They advised their patients on exercise and diet, prescribed herbal remedies that could be bought in herbalists' shops (above) and did basic operations (instruments below). Sick people also appealed to magic and the gods, particularly to Asclepius, the god of healing. Patients who slept in his temples expected him to appear in their dreams with miraculous cures. Surgery was performed without anaesthetics, and women often died during childbirth.

151

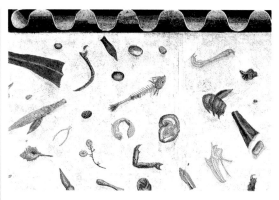

FOOD SCRAPS
This mosaic on a dining-room floor cleverly copies the debris from dinner. Guests would discard wishbones, fishbones, shells, lobsters' claws and fruit pits during the meal.

BANQUET BEHAVIOR
Men and women ate together at Roman banquets. Guests dressed in their best clothing, but removed their shoes once inside the host's house. Diners reclined three to a couch and ate mostly with their fingers. They drank wine mixed with water.

BIRDS FOR DINNER
Artists studied animals carefully and reproduced their behavior in accurate detail. In this mosaic, a cat is about to dine on a plump bird.

COOKING POTS
Cooking pots had to be strong because they were used frequently. Large pans (top center) rested on iron grids above hot coals.

SERVING BOY
The children of slaves also became slaves. The luckier ones worked indoors in private homes and helped to prepare food.

COOKING WITHOUT TOMATOES
There were many imported foods at banquets. But tomatoes did not reach Italy until the sixteenth century, after they were discovered in the Americas.

Food and Feasts

Romans ate their main meal of the day late in the afternoon. Lower classes had wheat and barley porridge, bread, vegetables, olives and grapes, and made cheap cuts of meat into sausages, rissoles and pies. Emperors arranged for hand-outs of grain and oil to the very poor. If grain deliveries were delayed, riots sometimes broke out in Rome. The emperor Tiberius warned the Senate that stopping the corn dole would mean "the utter ruin of the state." Unlike the poor, wealthy citizens ate extremely well. There was a saying in imperial Rome that the rich fell ill from overeating and the poor from not eating enough. Slaves from the East, who were skilled in preparing exotic dishes, were in great demand as cooks. Hosts spent huge sums of money on food for a banquet, which might last well into the night. The meal had three courses, each consisting of a range of dishes served on pottery, glass or even silver or gold platters.

BANQUET DISHES

Roman cook books listed dishes that required hours of preparation. Fish sauce, made from sprats, fish intestines, olive oil and herbs, was fermented in the sun for three days. Cooks might prepare appetizers of sows' udders or jellyfish stuffed with salted sea urchins.

Main courses could include flamingo with dates, roast parrot, boiled ostrich, and dormice stuffed with pork and pine nuts. Romans liked fruit for dessert, and army generals competed with one another to bring back new fruits from the provinces.

POORLY PROTECTED
These terra-cotta figurines are models of gladiators. Although they are wearing Thracian helmets, the rest of their scanty clothing leaves parts of their body dangerously exposed.

THE NET MAN
Unlike other gladiators, who wore some protective armor, the almost naked retiarius carried only a weighted net, a Neptune's trident used by tuna fishermen and a short sword.

THE ROAR OF THE CROWD
Several pairs of gladiators might fight at the same time: Samnite against Samnite (below), armed with sword and shield; Thracian against Samnite (center); and retiarius against Samnite (right). The audience cheered winners and booed losers loudly.

• LIVING IN THE EMPIRE •

Spectator Sports

Emperors and provincial governors arranged chariot races and violent games to amuse people on the frequent public holidays. People of all classes flocked eagerly to these entertainments. Rome's Circus Maximus was always packed on race days, when chariots thundered round the track to the deafening noise made by 260,000 onlookers. Most charioteers were slaves and the successful ones earned freedom. Convicts and slaves (both men and women) trained as gladiators. Equipped in the styles of warriors, such as Samnites and Thracians, or armed with fishing gear, they fought each other and wild animals, while musicians played bronze horns and water organs. Rome's amphitheater, known as the Colosseum, seated 60,000 spectators. The contestants shouted, "We who are about to die, salute you!" as they filed past the imperial stand during opening parades. Wounded gladiators could appeal for mercy, but jeers from the crowd and the thumbs-down signal from the referee brought death. Victorious gladiators were treated as stars and won their freedom.

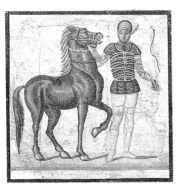

CHARIOTEERS' COLORS
In Rome, there were four important chariot teams—Reds, Blues, Whites and Greens (above). Every team had a large group of fans. Sometimes fights broke out between the different groups.

DID YOU KNOW?
One of the games staged in Rome on orders from the emperor Trajan lasted for 117 days. More than 10,000 gladiators took part.

FIRST PAST THE POST
Chariots were drawn by teams of two, three or four horses (left). Charioteers fell frequently during the race. First place went to the winning chariot, either with or without a driver.

154

GOING TO THE THEATER

Roman plays, which at first were translations from the Greek, included tragedies and comedies. Like the Greeks, Roman dramatic actors were male and wore masks (above). The audiences, who voiced their opinions noisily, preferred comedies. The most famous comedies were written by Plautus and Terence. The Romans developed comic mimes, which were performed without masks or words on rough stages in the streets. Women acted in these mimes. Because large-scale dramas were not as popular as other entertainments, some of the huge stone theaters later became gladiatorial arenas.

Roads and Travel

Roman roads, constructed by the army and slave laborers, carried soldiers, messengers, travelers and traders across the Empire. These straight, level highways followed the most direct routes, tunneling through hills and bridging rivers. They formed a network that allowed troops to march quickly to any trouble spot, and connected towns, cities and ports with Rome, the capital and center of government. Road construction usually began with digging a ditch about 3 ft (1 m) deep. This was filled with sand, and then with small stones and gravel mixed with concrete. Paving stones were laid on top and milestones set in place to mark distances. Roman roads were crammed with all kinds of people and animals. The rich traveled in carriages with several slaves. They sometimes slept in their vehicles or in tents pitched by the roadside because they were frightened of being robbed at the inns. Some roads lasted for many centuries and many present-day European roads follow old Roman routes.

HARBOR SCENE
The Romans built deep harbors like this one, which is probably in the Bay of Naples, so that goods and passengers could be loaded and unloaded safely onto ships.

MEASURED BY MILESTONES
Inscriptions in Roman numbers on low pillars of stone, placed at the edges of roads, told travelers the distances between towns.

DID YOU KNOW?

Road transport was slow and therefore expensive. Horses were faster than bullocks, but the Romans had no harnesses that allowed horses to pull heavy wagons. Horses were ridden or used to pull light carts.

HIGHWAY ONE

The first Roman road, built in 312 BC, linked Rome to Capua in southern Italy. It was called the Via Appia and later extended even farther south to present-day Brindisi.

TOURING THE EMPIRE

Many Roman tourists visited the Seven Wonders of the World, such as the Egyptian pyramids at Giza (left), and other places in the Empire. There were even some maps and guidebooks available. A few sightseers left lasting evidence of their travels in Latin graffiti on stone monuments in Egypt. Travelers often asked soothsayers to read the future before they began what might be a dangerous adventure. Robbers ambushed tourists on Italian roads, and barbarians attacked them in foreign lands. Sea voyagers ran into pirates and foul weather.

ROADSIDE INNS

During long journeys travelers often stopped to eat and sleep at inns beside the road. Surviving accounts of people's journeys tell us that these inns frequently served poor food and bad water. The noisy behavior of some of the guests often kept others awake.

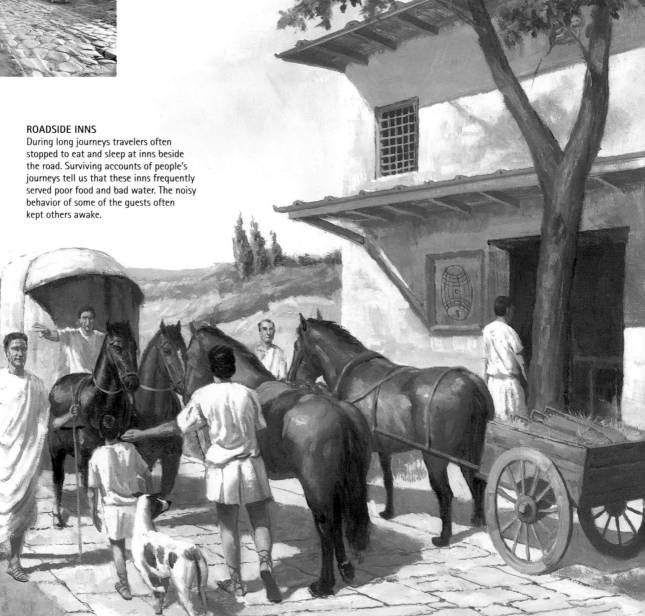

On the March

The conquests of ancient Rome depended on its well-trained army—a powerful fighting force that marched across much of the known world pushing out the Empire's frontiers. At first, only Roman men of property were allowed to serve as soldiers. Then, at the end of the second century BC, General Gaius Marius reformed the army and let citizens without property join. Many poor townsmen signed on for a period of up to 25 years. Military life was tough and punishments were harsh, but when soldiers retired, they were given money or a small plot of land to farm. By Julius Caesar's time, Rome had a highly efficient, wage-earning, permanent army. It was divided into 60 units, or legions, of foot soldiers called legionaries. Augustus later reduced the number of legions to 28 units. Legionaries were supported by auxiliary soldiers who were recruited mostly from the provinces. They formed infantry units (on foot) or cavalry units (on horseback).

MILITARY MONUMENT
Soldiers who died in battle were buried with honor. This monument to Gaius Musius, a standard-bearer of the 14th Legion, was erected by his brother.

MUSEUM PIECES
Many museums in Europe have collections of Roman military equipment. This cavalryman's ceremonial helmet is on display in London's British Museum.

MILITARY EQUIPMENT
A bronze cheek guard (top), an iron spear and javelin head, and the handle from a helmet were found at a fort in England. They were once used by Roman soldiers.

GUARDING THE EMPEROR
The Praetorian Guard, numbering about 9,000 soldiers, was the only part of the army stationed in Rome. Augustus formed this unit to protect the emperor and Italy.

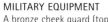

Section of a cohort

THE ROMAN LEGION

A Roman legion consisted of about 5,000 foot soldiers. The legion was divided into nine groups, called cohorts, of equal size, which were led by a tenth, larger cohort. Cohorts were split into six centuries. A century originally contained 100 men, but this number was later reduced to 80 to make the group easier to manage. Centuries were divided into groups of eight soldiers who shared a tent and ate together. Each legion carried a silver eagle into battle. If the eagle fell into enemy hands, the legion was disbanded.

GOING TO WAR
Each group of soldiers, called a century, was commanded by a centurion (front left) and had its own standard-bearer (front center). Legionaries marched with all their equipment and belongings. Besides their weapons, legionaries carried food for three days and tools for making camp, digging canals, laying roads and building bridges.

Q: What happened if a legion's silver eagle fell into enemy hands?

DID YOU KNOW?
Regular army pay attracted Rome's poorer citizens into the army. A salt allowance, called a salarium, formed part of a soldier's rations. The English word salary, describing payment of wages, comes from this Latin word "salarium."

RED SLIPWARE
Potteries in Gaul, Italy and Asia Minor produced huge amounts of red tableware. These fine drinking cups show the uniformity of shapes used throughout the Empire.

PORTRAIT OF THE DEAD
When the Romans invaded Egypt, Egyptian artists were influenced by Roman styles. They began to paint more lifelike portraits, such as this, on mummy cases.

• EXPANSION AND EMPIRE •

Growing Empire

Rome's frontiers began to expand long before imperial times. By 264 BC, the Romans dominated the whole of Italy and, after successful wars, ruled the island of Sardinia, territory in Spain and southwest Europe, and Carthage in North Africa. Roman government took hold in Greece in 146 BC, and during the next century, Rome's boundaries extended to the eastern Mediterranean. In 31 BC, before he became emperor, Augustus finally conquered Egypt. The emperor Claudius overran Mauretania and Thrace, and ordered the invasion of Britain. The emperor Trajan extended the Empire farthest with the conquests of Dacia and large areas of the Middle East. This expansion was later abandoned by his successor Hadrian (above left). Rome divided its territories into provinces, which were governed by senators. Several emperors were born in the provinces. Trajan, for example, came from Spain and Septimius Severus from Africa. Syria and Asia Minor were among Rome's richest provinces, for in those days good crops grew in what is now desert.

HADRIAN'S WALL
The emperor Hadrian ordered the army to build a wall in Britain at the northernmost boundary of Roman territory. Hadrian's Wall, about 75 miles (120 km) long, wound across the country near the present Scottish border. The wall, built mainly between AD 122 and 129, linked 14 forts and was intended to keep out invaders. Parts of the wall still stand.

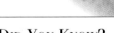

MILDENHALL TREASURE
This large dish, found at Mildenhall in Suffolk, England, is one of the finest surviving pieces of silverware from ancient Roman times. The central motif represents a sea god. The outer frieze shows followers of Bacchus.

DID YOU KNOW?
The provinces paid taxes to Rome but were not governed by Roman law. Laws, which took into account local customs, were made for each province added to the Empire.

160

THE PAX ROMANA

From the time of Augustus (left), Roman legions stationed on the frontiers kept the Pax Romana—the peace of Rome. This meant that country people within the borders of the Empire could cultivate their land and raise stock without fear of invasion. The Pax Romana benefited townspeople, too, by protecting trade routes across the Empire. A well-to-do family in Britain, for example, could drink Greek wine from glasses made in Syria and eat from silverware crafted in France.

The Beginnings of Christianity

IN THE ROUND
This mosaic comes from the floor of a Roman villa in Hinton St. Mary in Dorset, England. It is the earliest picture of Jesus Christ in Britain.

BEARDED CHRIST
This fourth-century painting is on the ceiling of Commodile Cemetery in Rome. Here, Jesus Christ has a beard as he does in most later Christian art.

Jesus, a carpenter by trade, lived in Nazareth, a village in the province of Judaea. When he was 27 or 28 years old, he began preaching to a growing band of followers. These people believed Jesus was chosen by their god to lead them. Some years later, Pontius Pilate, the Roman governor, declared Jesus a rebel against the state and ordered him to be crucified under Roman law. His death inspired the spread of the Christian religion throughout the Empire. Two of Jesus' followers, Peter and Paul, took this new religion to Rome. In its early years, Christianity was very popular with slaves and the poor because it promised everlasting life, regardless of wealth. The Christian belief in one god conflicted with the Roman state religion and with the official view that the emperors were gods. Because Christians would not take part in the ceremonies on special festival days of emperor worship, they were cruelly punished. They were forced to meet secretly.

GOING UNDERGROUND
When the Romans refused to allow the Christians to bury their dead in official burial places, the Christians dug large passages, called catacombs, beneath uninhabited sections of Rome and Naples, and under some cities in Sicily and North Africa. They placed the shrouded bodies in openings along the walls, which they often decorated with paintings.

CATACOMB PAINTING
Early paintings of Jesus Christ, such as this one on the wall of a catacomb, often showed him as a short-haired, beardless young man in the role of the Good Shepherd.

TOMB INSCRIPTION
This inscription from Rome's catacombs dates from the third century. It is simpler than most tomb inscriptions and may have been carved secretly and in haste.

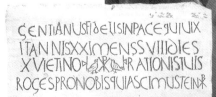

THE EDICT OF MILAN

Christianity soon attracted followers both rich and poor. It spread so rapidly that by 311 the emperor Galerius passed a law allowing Christians to worship openly "on condition they in no way act against the established order." Two years later, the Edict of Milan issued by the emperor Constantine I gave Christians the freedom to inherit and dispose of property, and to elect their own church government. Constantine I (above) was baptised as a Christian shortly before he died in 337. In 380, under Theodosius I, Christianity became the official religion of the Empire.

THE GOOD SHEPHERD
This fine statue of Jesus Christ as the Good Shepherd is remarkable because it was made in secret at a time when Christianity was still generally forbidden.

Empire in Decline

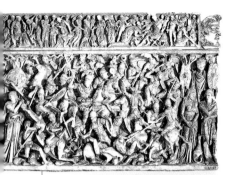

BATTLING THE BARBARIANS
Scenes from battles were often carved on large stone coffins, known as sarcophagi. This one belonged to a general who fought in the Germanic wars in Marcus Aurelius's army.

DID YOU KNOW?

Diocletian sent out officials to count the Empire's population. They brought back detailed information. The census counted everything from people to livestock and olive trees.

The huge Roman Empire was difficult and expensive to run. From AD 161 to 180, the emperor Marcus Aurelius had to fight many campaigns to protect the boundaries. By the third century AD, the army was stretched too far and taxes were raised to cover the Empire's costs. Farmers who could not afford the taxes abandoned their farms, and cities suffered as the economy slumped and their markets declined. Many emperors were weak, so generals competed for power. Civil wars raged, and barbarians, sensing the Empire's weakness, attacked the frontiers. Diocletian (above left) became emperor in AD 284. He split the Empire in order to make it easier to manage, appointing Maximian to rule the West, and keeping the wealthier East for himself. Diocletian also reorganized the army and the provinces. Soon after Diocletian and Maximian retired in 305, civil wars broke out again until Constantine took power over the whole Empire in 324. He moved the imperial court to Byzantium, which he renamed Constantinople.

TRIUMPHAL ARCH

The Arch of Constantine was built to celebrate a victory at the Battle of the Milvian Bridge near Rome in 312. Many of the arch's best carvings were stolen from second-century monuments.

COLLECTING TAXES

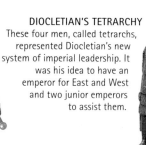

Emperors needed huge sums of money to support the large army and pay for their extravagant lifestyles, expensive works of art, large building programs and the corn dole. This revenue was raised through taxation. People had to pay taxes on land, slaves, crops, roads and goods from shops. Tax officials (above) were required to collect set amounts of money and had to make up any shortfall from their own wages. They were harsh and unfeeling about collecting what was owed.

DIOCLETIAN'S TETRARCHY

These four men, called tetrarchs, represented Diocletian's new system of imperial leadership. It was his idea to have an emperor for East and West and two junior emperors to assist them.

ATTILA THE HUN

The Huns were a barbarian tribe from central Asia. By 447, Attila, king of the Huns, and his large army of warriors had conquered all the countries between the Black Sea and the Mediterranean. They defeated the Roman army in three battles, but did not capture Constantinople and Rome.

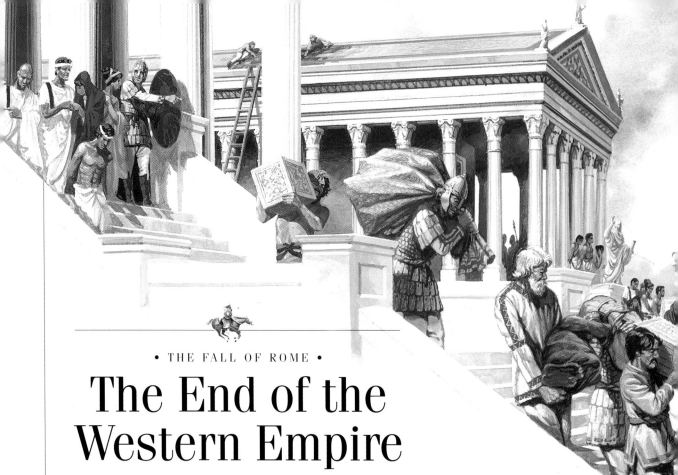

• THE FALL OF ROME •

The End of the Western Empire

The Romans, like the ancient Greeks, called all tribes whose language they could not understand "barbarians." The emperor Theodosius I allowed German barbarian tribes to settle in the north of the Empire when they were driven there by the fierce Asiatic Huns. But by the early fifth century, other barbarian people, including the Huns themselves, came looking for land to settle. They fought the imperial armies and the Germans, and soon occupied large areas that had once been Roman territory. After Theodosius I died in 395, the Western and Eastern Roman empires split forever in matters of government, but the West still depended upon the East for money and grain supplies. King Alaric led the Visigoths into Rome in 410 and became the first person to conquer the city in 800 years. The Vandals later plundered Rome in 455. The Eastern Empire refused to help the Western Empire, which finally ended in 476 when the last Western emperor, Romulus Augustulus, was exiled by the barbarians.

SACKING OF ROME
Gaiseric, leader of the barbarian Vandals, sailed to Ostia in AD 455. His soldiers entered Rome and spent 12 days stripping buildings of everything valuable, including the gilded roof tiles of important temples. Gaiseric took the widow of the emperor Valentinian III and her daughters hostage.

BESET BY BARBARIANS
Hordes of barbarians seeking land attacked the frontiers and swarmed into the Western Empire.

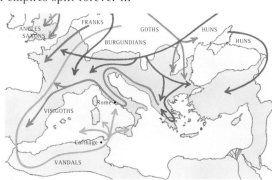

VILLAS FOR VANDALS

When the Vandals overran Roman territory in North Africa, local landowners faced slavery or exile. This mosaic from Carthage shows a Vandal in front of a Roman villa.

SAFE HARBOR

Ravenna became the Western Empire's capital in 402. The city was connected to the mainland by a causeway. Ships entering the harbor had to pass between lighthouse towers.

SPREADING CHRISTIANITY

The Christian Church survived when the Western Empire collapsed and Rome became the holiest of Western Christian cities. The first Christian monasteries were in Egypt, but soon monastic communities were formed throughout the former Western Empire. The monks preserved many ancient Roman manuscripts by patiently copying them out by hand. The symbol at right, called a Chi-Rho, was one of the earliest Christian symbols and is found on many Christian objects. It combines the first two letters of Christ's name in Greek.

PANEL PICTURE
The Byzantine Christians produced panel pictures called icons. They were often painted on wood, like this one of St. Gregory.

IVORY DIPTYCH
A carving in two panels is called a diptych. This ivory one from Constantinople, made in about 500, shows gladiators fighting lions in an arena.

SIGN OF VICTORY
Before winning the Battle of the Milvian Bridge, Constantine I claimed he saw a flaming cross and the words "In this conquer." The cross became a Christian symbol.

• THE FALL OF ROME •

Eastern Empire

The Empire in the East, which came to be known as the Byzantine Empire, prospered as the Western Empire weakened. The city of Constantinople grew wealthy. Its geographical position between Europe and Asia was good both for trade and for managing its territory. The frontiers of the Byzantine Empire extended west to Greece, south to Egypt, and east to the border with Arabia. Although Greek was the official language of the East, Latin was often still spoken at the emperor's court. During his rule from 527 to 565, Justinian (above left) regained some of the western provinces in Africa, Italy and Spain, but he did not hold them for long. Many other Eastern emperors had long reigns and governed well. The Byzantine Empire was never a great military power and tried to settle difficulties with its neighbors by peaceful means. Its people were Christians, and invaders who threatened the Empire were frequently persuaded to join it instead and become Christians, too.

EASTERN CAPITAL

Like Rome, Constantinople (left) covered seven hills. The emperor Constantine I began a grand building program to beautify Constantinople, which was protected by water on three sides. Later, a wall was built around the city by Theodosius II. Justinian I built Hagia Sophia, which was the largest Christian church of the time.

OTTOMAN TURKS

During the thirteenth century, the Ottoman Empire, which was located in what is now Turkey, began to expand its frontiers. The Ottoman Turks followed the Islamic religion and set out to conquer Christian cities. Gradually they controlled most of the Eastern Roman Empire. The troops of Sultan Mehmet II (above) besieged Constantinople for six weeks before the city finally fell in 1453. This was the end of the Byzantine Empire and Constantinople became known as Istanbul.

GOLDEN GIFT

The empress Theodora, Justinian's wife, was very generous to the Christian Church. Here, attended by her ladies-in-waiting, she presents a golden chalice to the Church of San Vitale in Ravenna, Italy.

169

Native Americans

- Why did some Native American babies have many names?

- What did Navajos use to cure stomach complaints?

- Why were buffalo so important to the Plains Indians?

Where Did They Come From?

Native Americans tell wonderful creation stories to explain where they came from. Some say Coyote shaped people from mud; others think Raven called them from a clam shell because he was lonely. Archaeologists, however, suggest people arrived in several groups, beginning at least 15,000 years ago, perhaps much earlier. The first Americans came from Asia and followed herds of grazing animals across a land bridge formed during the Ice Age, when the great glaciers sucked up the shallow seas and left dry land. Later, when the Earth began to warm, this land bridge disappeared and became the Bering Strait. The people trekked slowly southward into North America through a harsh landscape. They were excellent hunters and speared huge animals such as woolly mammoths and long-horned bison. These enormous beasts later died out, and the people were forced to hunt smaller game and collect wild plants for food.

TOOLS
Early Native Americans made knives from stone and bone, which were sharp enough to slice up large animals. They used scrapers to remove the fur and flesh from skins.

SHAMAN'S MASK
Many thousands of years ago, an Arctic woodcarver shaped this mask for a shaman (healer) to wear during the ceremonies that called upon the spirits to bring good health and good hunting.

CREATION STORY

The Northeastern Iroquois describe Skywoman's fall from her home. Water birds guided her to an island that a muskrat was building from mud and a turtle's shell. The island grew to become the Earth, and the world began when Skywoman gave birth to a daughter.

HUNTING AND FIGHTING
Early hunters and warriors flaked stone into deadly tips for their spears and lances. They made heavy war clubs from whale bone.

WALK ACROSS THE STRAIT
A strip of water called the Bering Strait now separates Siberia from Alaska. In the Ice Age, when the sea level dropped, the strait became a land bridge for herds of migrating game and the hunters who pursued them.

Siberia

Alaska

Land bridge

Glaciers

Where Did They Live?

Tribes of Native Americans spread across the land, depending on nature for food and shelter. Where they lived shaped the way they lived, and each group began to develop different customs and ways of doing things. On the rugged Northwest Coast, the "Salmon and Cedar People" built with wood and ate mainly fish, like their neighbors on the high Plateau. The Inuit (Eskimos) hunted polar bears across the treeless tundra and whales in freezing Arctic waters. Caribou provided nearly everything Subarctic families needed, while buffalo sustained the Plains Indians. In California, the mild climate meant that tribes there had plenty to eat, unlike the parched Great Basin where food was scarce. In the Northeast and Great Lakes, people traveled the rivers and cleared forest plots to grow corn and tobacco. Most Southwest and Southeast tribes became farmers and lived in villages.

Blackfoot medicine man from the Great Plains

Nootka woman from the Northwest Coast

Kalispel woman from the Plateau

Ute warrior from the Great Basin

Hupa man from California

Navajo youth from the Southwest

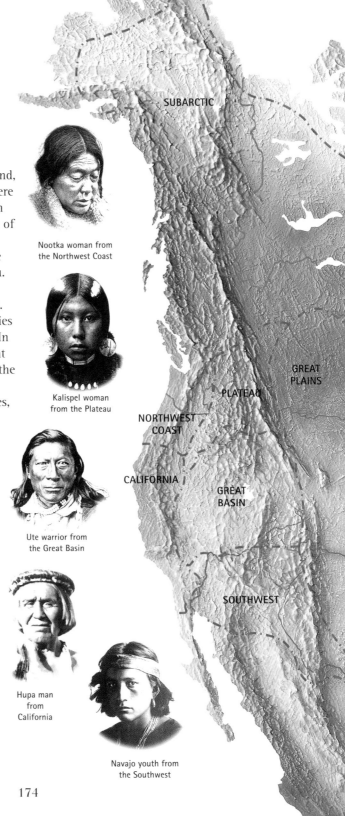

SUBARCTIC

GREAT PLAINS

PLATEAU

NORTHWEST COAST

CALIFORNIA

GREAT BASIN

SOUTHWEST

SOUTHWEST LANDSCAPE
A parade of saguaro cactuses in the dry Southwest provided nourishment when the fruit formed and ripened.

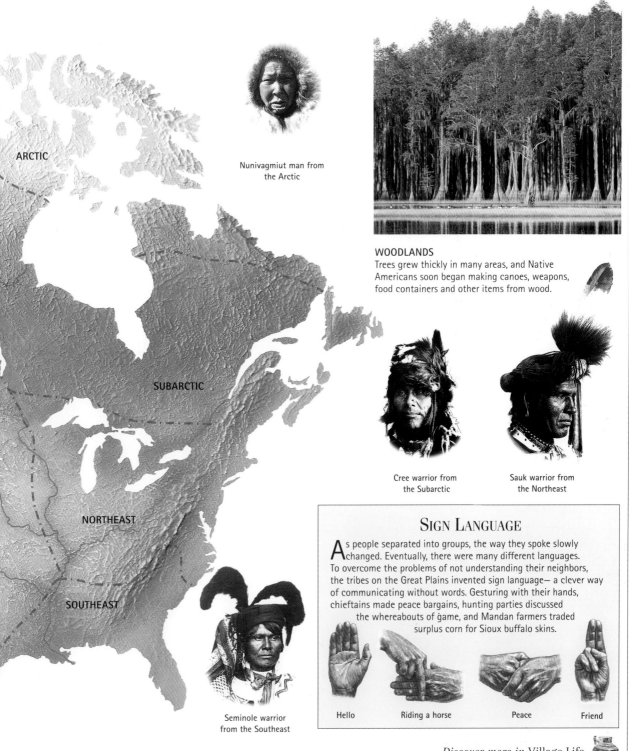

ARCTIC

Nunivagmiut man from
the Arctic

SUBARCTIC

NORTHEAST

SOUTHEAST

WOODLANDS
Trees grew thickly in many areas, and Native
Americans soon began making canoes, weapons,
food containers and other items from wood.

Cree warrior from
the Subarctic

Sauk warrior from
the Northeast

Seminole warrior
from the Southeast

SIGN LANGUAGE

As people separated into groups, the way they spoke slowly
changed. Eventually, there were many different languages.
To overcome the problems of not understanding their neighbors,
the tribes on the Great Plains invented sign language— a clever way
of communicating without words. Gesturing with their hands,
chieftains made peace bargains, hunting parties discussed
the whereabouts of game, and Mandan farmers traded
surplus corn for Sioux buffalo skins.

Hello   Riding a horse   Peace   Friend

Discover more in Village Life

What Did They Wear?

DRESSED FOR BEST
Both men and women wore ceremonial robes made from soft buckskin, decorated with fringe and porcupine quill embroidery. The brave's full-length war bonnet and coup stick are trimmed with ermine tails and eagle feathers. The feathers show his courage in hand-to-hand fighting.

Native Americans loved decorated ceremonial costumes, but had simple everyday clothes. They dressed to suit the weather on windy plains, in the chill Arctic, in damp rainforests, or in the dry desert, where often they wore very little. Most garments fitted loosely for easy movement—loincloths, shirts, tunics and leggings for men; skirts and dresses for women. In winter, people added shawls, blankets and extra clothing. They made garments from the things around them. Animals provided skins for cloth, sinews for thread and bones for needles. One moose could clothe a person in the Northeast, a single caribou supplied a jacket in the Subarctic, but a man's robe in the Great Basin required a hundred rabbit skins. Where game was scarce, the people wove cloth from plant material, such as nettle fiber and cedar bark.

SNOW GOGGLES
The Inuit (Eskimos) wore goggles shaped from walrus tusk. These protected their eyes from the intense glare of the sun reflected off the snow.

KEEPING WARM
Men, women and children dressed alike against the cold in waterproof pants, hooded parkas, boots and mittens. Caribou and seal skins with the fur turned inside were most popular. Here, the mother chews skin to soften it, while the father carves an ivory ornament with a bow drill.

BARK WEAVING
While her grandchild rocks gently in a cradle, this woman weaves a basket from dampened strips of cedar bark. Her clothing is also woven from shredded bark. Cedar bark was one of the main plant fibers used by the people of the Northwest Coast.

FOOTWEAR
Plains women stitched leather moccasins with hard or soft soles. They decorated them with dyed porcupine quills and elaborate beadwork.

CLOTHING MATERIALS

Native Americans made their clothing from the animal and plant materials they found around them.

Areas where animal fur (such as caribou, seal and polar bear) and hide (such as buckskin and buffalo) were used for clothing.

Areas where cotton was mainly used for clothing.

Areas where both animal skins and plant materials were used for clothing.

Discover more in Getting Around

177

Life as a Child

Children spent most of the first year of their lives strapped snugly in a cradleboard, carried everywhere by their mothers. Later, a large family of parents, aunts, uncles and grandparents watched over them and taught them tribal ways. Girls practiced preparing food, sewing, tanning hides, making pottery, basket weaving and embroidering with dyed porcupine quills. Boys learned to make tools and weapons and how to hunt and fight. There was always time for games, such as hurtling down snowy slopes on sleds made from buffalo ribs. When children reached puberty, there were important ceremonies, sometimes with dancing, special clothes and the gift of a new name. Apache girls were showered with yellow tule pollen; Alaskan girls had their faces tattooed. After puberty, girls joined the women in the tribe, but boys had to pass tests of courage, such as wounding or killing an enemy, before they could become true hunters and warriors.

UMBILICAL POUCHES
Some tribes sewed newborn babies' umbilical cords into beaded pouches shaped like lizards or turtles. They believed these creatures would bless their infants with long life.

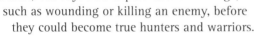

TARGET PRACTICE
Sioux boys learned how to use small bows and arrows, shooting first at still targets and then at moving jack rabbits.

UNDER THE STARS
Like Native American children everywhere, the boys and girls of the Great Basin gathered to hear stories. The retelling of myths, legends and folktales taught the children tribal history and customs.

DRESSING WARM
St. Lawrence Island children in the Arctic wore parkas made from reindeer skin with the hairy side on the inside. The tops of boys' heads were shaved like the men of the tribe. Girls kept their hair long.

A baby's name was very important, but it was often chosen by relatives and tribal elders, not by the parents. When a Southwest Hopi baby was 20 days old, the father's mother and his sisters visited with many blessings and suggested names. Inuit (Eskimos) gave newborn infants another name every time they cried, so some tiny babies had dozens of names. A Seminole boy was rewarded with a new name when he proved his courage in battle.

Seminole child

CRADLEBOARD
This Cheyenne cradleboard was made of beaded cotton lashed securely to a wooden frame. It fitted comfortably on the mother's back.

BRIDAL NECKLACE
A Zuni man made this silver and turquoise necklace for his daughter. The traditional squash blossom design represented a mother surrounded by her many children.

• THE PEOPLE •

Choosing a Partner

Some Native American couples began life together with a simple exchange of presents. Then the girl (perhaps no more than 13 years old) moved into her husband's home, or he joined her family. Subarctic partners set up a wigwam together. Marriage ceremonies varied greatly between tribes and regions. The richest of the Northwest Coast Tlingits gave huge wedding feasts and valuable presents. A Plains boy courted his sweetheart with fluted love tunes. In the evening, outside her tepee, the couple hid from curious passers-by with a blanket over their heads, while they chatted to see if they liked each other. In later times, wealthy Plains bridegrooms gave horses to the bride's family. Southwestern Hopis sealed their marriage partnership when the mothers washed their hair together in one bowl.

WISHRAM BRIDE
A Wishram bride on the high Plateau wore wedding finery made from panels of dentalium shells, edged with beads and coins.

READY FOR MARRIAGE
A Hopi girl's elaborate hairstyle indicated to a Hopi boy that she was old enough to be married.

MARRIAGE DOLLS
Menominee newlyweds near the Great Lakes received a pair of dolls as a wedding present. These were "good medicine" for a long and happy marriage.

ACROSS THE WATER
This Kwakiutl bride arrived at her future husband's village in the family canoe.

WEDDING BASKETS
Navajo wedding baskets always belonged to the bride. When a man moved into his wife's home, he looked after her goods but never owned them himself.

READY FOR MARRIAGE
A Hopi boy wore several fine bead necklaces on his wedding day.

HOPI WEDDING
A Hopi bride ground corn for three days in her chosen partner's house to show her wifely skills. After the hair-washing ceremony, she stayed there while the groom and his male relatives wove her wedding clothes. Then she walked home in one outfit, carrying the second one in a reed container. Women were buried in their wedding garments so that when they entered the spirit world, they would be properly dressed.

Wedding blanket sash

Games and Sport

Many tribes played stickball or lacrosse (shown here) to settle quarrels and to ask the spirits to send rain or to heal a sick person. The game was fast and violent, and players in the Southeast called it "the little brother of war." Competitors were sometimes severely injured or even killed during the game. The spectators chanted and cheered to urge the players on and bet furs, skins and trinkets on the results. Sports helped the men develop their hunting and fighting skills, such as strength, courage, staying power, swiftness and keenness of eye. As well as team games, there were running, canoe and horse races, spear throwing and archery contests. In some tribes, women also played active sports. But most of all, people throughout the land loved to gamble. Games of chance included guessing which way up peach kernels or walnut shells would land in a bowl, which hand held a marked bone or which moccasin contained a small stone.

PLAYING CARDS
Both Apache men and women enjoyed card games. The packs of cards were cut from rawhide and painted with bold designs.

DID YOU KNOW?
Sioux women bet on the fall of dice made from bones, beavers' teeth and other materials, which were carved and painted with spiders, lizards or turtles.

ARCTIC KICKBALL
Arctic tribes played kickball with a leather ball stuffed with caribou fur.

PLAYING PATOL

Patol is a game of chance played by two to four people. They use counters called "horses," stick dice and stones arranged in a circle or rectangle. Players become very skilful at throwing the dice. Patol was popular in the Southwest, where games took place outside in front of interested onlookers.

RING AND PIN
In this game, players held the wooden pin and tried to pass the loop of string over the deer-foot bones.

GAMBLING GAME
The sticks in this game were shuffled under a cover and divided into two bundles. Players then guessed which bundle contained a specially marked stick.

Hoop

Lance

HOOP AND POLE GAME
This was a game of great skill. Competitors had to throw a lance through a hoop as it rolled along the ground. A hit on the center hole scored the most points.

Canoes and Kayaks

People built boats for fishing, moving between hunting grounds, carrying goods and going to war. Some hollowed out massive tree trunks with fire, others wove crafts from reeds, or covered wooden frames with birch bark and sealed the seams with hot black spruce gum. Low-ended crafts steered best in calm waters. Boats with high bows and sterns resisted rough waves and were more suitable for the open ocean. The tall prow of a ceremonial Northwest Coast canoe (shown here) was carved and painted to reflect the family's importance. The fearsome bear is a villager dressed in his winter dance costume. The Californian Chumash put to sea in canoes built from pine planks. Inuit (Eskimos) made lightweight, waterproof kayaks, by stretching oiled animal skins over driftwood frames. Most kayaks were for one person, though some held two.

LONG BOAT
It took 11 men to launch this canoe, which was carved from a single tree trunk.

HUNTING CRAFT
Inuit hunters stalked sea mammals in their speedy, silent kayaks.

PADDLE POWER

The helmsman used a broad-bladed oar. The crew propelled the boat through the water with shorter, more pointed blades. Patterns on the paddles matched the canoe's decoration.

TULE BOAT

In Northern California, fishers skimmed across the lakes in boats made from bundles of tule reeds, lashed together. These reeds grew plentifully near water.

BIRCH BARK CANOE

Sheets of paper birch bark, sewn together, formed the best covering. The resin in the bark stopped it from stretching or shrinking.

MAKING A DUGOUT CANOE

Northwest Coast people used the sea as both hunting ground and trade route. They built one kind of canoe for the calmer waters of the bay and another for the open ocean.

The cedar log was split lengthwise. Shaping began with a stone tool.

The sides were chipped away to reach the required thickness.

Hollowing the inside to the correct thickness took skill and time.

Water heated with hot rocks softened the wood. Thwarts were fitted to broaden the interior.

The bow and stern pieces were attached, and the hull was sanded and decorated.

TOY CANOE

This birch bark model is engraved all over, unlike a full-sized canoe, which was not decorated on the bottom.

BULLBOAT

Mandan women rowed bullboats made from buffalo hides stretched over frames of willow.

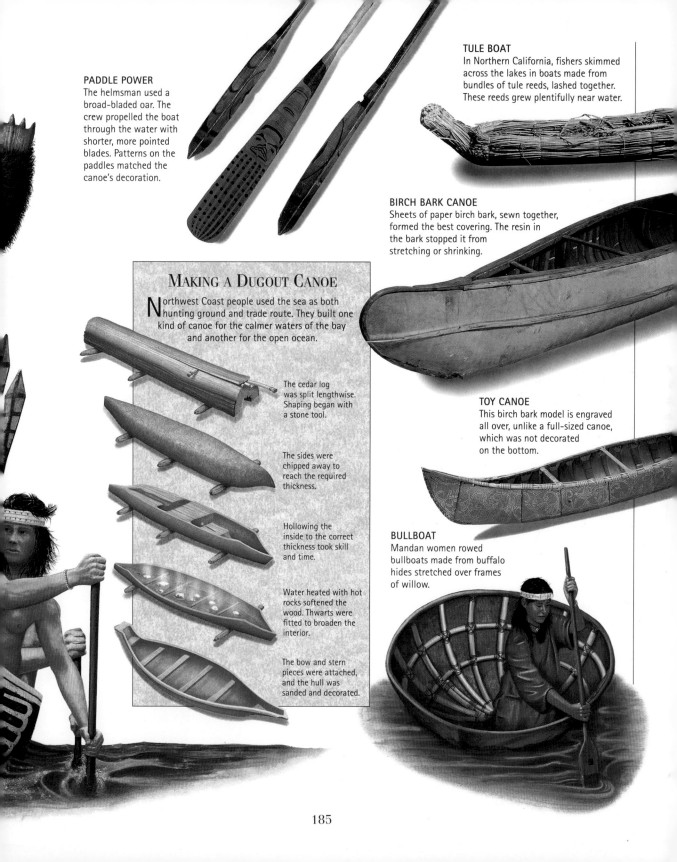

185

DOG SLEDDING

The inventive Arctic tribes trained huskies to pull sleds. They laid a platform of driftwood or caribou antlers on wooden or whalebone runners. The Netsilik sometimes used rolled animal skins for runners, with frozen fish as crosspieces— a handy food supply in the spring thaw.

• ON THE MOVE •

Getting Around

Native Americans walked huge distances in their never-ending quest for food. Apaches painted their moccasins with sacred tule pollen because they believed it would help them find their way. Possessions had to be carried, and woven baskets were popular containers. A broad band, called a tumpline, held the load on the back of the human carrier. Women took the heaviest burdens and backpacked babies, tied tightly in slings or cradleboards. Men seldom carried anything but weapons, because they always had to be ready to hunt or to defend the group. The Subarctic people hauled packs on toboggans. In other places, people harnessed dogs to wooden travois or loaded them with parfleches. Later, horses and pack ponies made life easier for the tribes who had them.

PIGGYBACKING

Young children, like this Hopi toddler, rode on their mother's back. This was a comfortable and safe way of carrying them for long distances where there were no sleds or toboggans.

TANGLE FREE

Ivory separators and swivels kept harness lines on dog sleds from becoming tangled.

DOG TRAVOIS

A tough dog could pull a load about equal in weight to two medium-sized suitcases full of clothes.

SNOWSHOE SHUFFLE

Snowshoes, shaped like bear paws or beaver tails, were the perfect winter footwear for journeying through deep snow drifts. They allowed hunters to keep pace with caribou and other large game without their feet sinking into the soft snow. Subarctic tribes laced bent frames of birchwood with strips of wet caribou hide. When the webbing dried, it was tight and light.

PLAIN AND SIMPLE

The Southeastern Seminoles made their moccasins from a single piece of soft buckskin gathered at the seam.

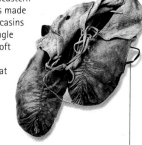

WALKING WARM

In summer, Eskimos gathered grasses and braided them into socks. They were shaped to fit the foot snugly.

HUSKY HELPERS

Husky dogs pulled sleds in teams. They also used their keen noses to track down seals for the hunters.

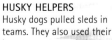

Discover more in Tepees

Horses and Ponies

SADDLE BLANKET
Respected horses were as
well-dressed as their owners.
It took many hours to edge
this blanket with beads.

Horses brought speed to the Plains Indians and changed
their hunting and fighting ways. They were called "Spirit
Dogs" or "Medicine Dogs," but were much stronger and
faster pack animals than real dogs. With horses, whole settlements
could move freely to follow the buffalo. The hunter–warrior had
a special bond with his horse; only he trained and rode it,
bathed it in summer, covered it with buffalo skins in winter
and tethered it beside his tepee. Horses, extinct since the Ice
Age, were reintroduced by the Spanish in the sixteenth century
and spread gradually from tribe to tribe. The Plains
Comanches excelled in taming wild horses. Comanche women
joined the men on antelope hunts, and the children rode solo
by the age of five. Plateau tribes bred Appaloosa horses
and Indian ponies and became expert horse traders.

WHIPS AND QUIRTS
Whips or quirts urged horses
on. This quirt is made
from an elk antler
and a leather strip.

STRANGERS ON HORSEBACK

This Navajo cave painting of a Spanish friar and his companions has survived from the sixteenth century.

SADDLE UP

Men usually rode bareback. Women used saddles and stirrups. Crow women spent many hours trimming theirs with beads.

Saddle pommel

Stirrup

SADDLE BAG

Bags were made from deerskin, stitched up the sides. They were tied to the pommel of the saddle.

BATTLEDRESS

Plains warriors depended on their war horses. The animals' reactions in battle could mean the difference between life and death. They had to endure the noise, move quickly, turn sharply and respond instantly to their riders' commands. Warriors shared battle honors with their mounts and painted them with the symbols they used on their own bodies (below). The horses wore eagle feathers and scalp locks, and their manes and tails were often trimmed and dyed.

Plains pony

Appaloosa horse

War party leader

Enemy killed in hand combat

Hail

Mourning marks

TAILPIECE

A crupper passed from the back of the saddle under the horse's tail to keep the saddle from slipping.

Discover more in Life on a Reservation

The Foragers

From early spring to late autumn, many Native American tribes moved around frequently, searching for things to eat. They foraged for seeds, berries, nuts and roots. In the Great Basin, March cattail shoots were the first fresh vegetables, while September's pine nuts provided needed stores for winter. Occasional grasshopper plagues were tasty feasts. The men caught almost anything, from rats, mice, caterpillars and lizards, to larger game including jack rabbits and deer. They made lifelike decoys from reeds and feathers to lure wild ducks into shallow water. Then they grabbed the birds or shot them down with arrows. In California, foragers hunted in the mountains and on the sea coast. They harvested acorns from oak trees and ground them into flour.

SEED HARVESTING
When the seeds ripened, Californian women beat them straight from the bushes into their carrying baskets.

THE RIPE TIME

The summer sun ripened fruits, nuts and berries, and tribes knew where to find them in their region. The foragers dried some of these and put them aside for winter, when food was often in very short supply.

Persimmons

Cranberries

Black walnut

Buffalo berries

Pine nuts

WICKER LARDER
The foragers used woven baskets to collect, store and carry food. These were much lighter than containers made from clay and were not easily broken.

A DIFFICULT CATCH
The sure-footed bighorn sheep that browsed in the desert mountains provided a satisfying meal. Men, women and children banded together to trap the animals.

Club

**HALIBUT
FISHING TACKLE**
The Tlingits carved hooks
to catch halibut. They
stunned the heavy fish
with clubs before hauling
them into the boat.

Hook

HARPOONING WALRUSES
Hunting walruses was
dangerous but worthwhile.
They provided meat, skin
for boats and clothing,
and ivory tusks for
ornaments and utensils.

• MAKING A LIVING •

The Fishers

In late spring, salmon begin to race up the inland waterways
to lay their eggs. The Northwestern tribes thought they came
especially to provide their people with food, and caught them
in nets and traps. They offered prayers to the first salmon landed,
roasted it for everyone to taste, and returned the whole skeleton
to the river where, they believed, it would come alive again. The
ocean was also a rich source of food for these people. From it,
they took whales, seals, huge halibut, cod and sturgeon, all kinds
of shellfish and oily candlefish, which gave them fuel for lamps.
Other tribes speared fish by torchlight from their canoes on the
Great Lakes and used nets and traps during the day. In parts of the
Southeast, the people depended on fish, as well as turtles,
alligators and deer, for protein in their diet. The Inuit (Eskimos)
needed meat from sea mammals to survive in winter when they
had no plant food. They caught seals and stalked walruses
among the ice floes.

DID YOU KNOW?
The Inuit (Eskimos) divided their world
into land and sea things. They would not
eat the flesh of land and sea animals in
the same meal or cook caribou meat
over a driftwood fire.

NET GAUGE
Twine to make mesh fishing nets was wound around a rectangular gauge. This one is made from elk antlers.

WHALING IN A UMIAK

Whales were dangerous prey. Arctic tribes went after them in single-sailed rowing boats called umiaks. They were made from whalebone covered with walrus hides and waterproofed with seal oil. Umiaks were much stronger than kayaks. Inuit (Eskimo) fishers sometimes hunted bowhead whales that were twice as long as the boats. They caught smaller beluga whales for their skin and tusked narwhals for their oil.

Whaling float

TRAPPING FISH
The Ingalik people of the Subarctic set wheel fish traps beneath the ice. Large ones, like this, were mainly used for snaring ling, a cod-like fish.

ULU KNIFE
Women butchered meat, scraped skins and cut leather with an ulu. It had a slate blade and a bone, ivory or wood handle.

Discover more in Canoes and Kayaks

Making a Meal

Imagine making a meal with no tap water, no gas or electricity and no refrigeration and supermarkets. Native Americans had none of these, and the women spent hours collecting food and water and preparing things to eat. Their daughters worked alongside them from a very early age. Pueblo women baked corn bread in outdoor ovens. The Northwestern Tlingits filled baskets of closely woven spruce roots with water, meat and vegetables, dropped in hot stones till the water boiled, and made a stew. Plains Indians used buffalo-hide containers in the same way. Metal cooking pots, which lasted much longer than skin or woven ones, became popular after tribes began trading with the Europeans. Native Americans had no set meal times. People ate when they were hungry, after a good hunt or when travelers arrived. Sharing was very important. Plenty of food meant lots for everyone. If provisions were in short supply, the small amounts were divided evenly. Most tribes stored food for the winter, when plants and game were harder to find.

PLENTY ON THE PLAINS
During most of the year, there was plenty to eat on the Plains. These Cheyenne women are pounding wild cherries and cooking with hot stones and metal pots. Turnips and squash will be added to the stew.

DRYING CHILIES
Chili peppers were a popular crop in the Southwest and gave the food a hot, spicy flavor. The pods were strung on plant fibers or cotton cords and hung up to dry.

SUN-DRIED FOODS
When food was plentiful, it could be preserved for winter. Fish, meat, corn, fruit and vegetables were hung on racks or spread out on platforms to dry in the sun.

IN STORAGE
Large storage jars for food were woven from willow wood and sedge roots. They were patterned with darker plants, such as devil's claw, or decorated with brightly colored feathers.

GRINDING CORN

Most days young Hopi women gathered to grind corn. They placed the corn kernels on a rough stone slab called a "metate" and rubbed them with a smaller stone called a "mano." Then they moved the pieces to progressively smoother slabs and crushed them into finer and finer particles. The Hopi cooked cornmeal flour in several ways. They made it into more than 30 different dishes including bread, gruel, pancakes and dumplings.

Discover more in Village Life

195

Village Life

Living in villages meant safety in numbers and shared supplies. Some groups built permanent dwellings. Others followed the food trails, like the Subarctic people who carried caribou skin shelters from camp to camp. Several tribes wintered in pit houses covered with mud. Alaskan Eskimos lived partly underground beneath turf roofs, while Southeastern Seminoles raised their thatched homes on stilts above the swampy land. Southwesterners solved the problem of fitting many people into a small space by stacking their stone and mud-brick houses one on top of another, like modern apartment buildings. Native American dwellings came in various shapes: cones, domes, triangles, squares and rectangles. Their names were just as varied: chickees, hogans, igloos, tepees, longhouses, lean-tos, wigwams and wickiups.

ROUND HOUSES
The Mandan people built villages on rises beside the Missouri River. Heavy rain ran easily down the domed sides of the houses.

PUEBLO VILLAGE
Southwestern villages were honeycombs of two-storey stone houses. Ladders led to the roofs and the entrances to the upper rooms.

SPLIT LEVEL LIVING
Up to 12 Northeastern Iroquois families shared a longhouse. The top level was used for storage, the bottom for sleeping. Curtains separated areas.

VILLAGE LAYOUT

In the well-planned Creek villages of the Southeast, airy summer sleepouts were built beside warmer lodges. The largest round council buildings could seat 500 people. The villagers used them for ceremonies, dancing, winter meetings of the tribal elders and to house the homeless and the aged.

FRONT DOOR POLES
Northwest Coast tribes, such as the Haida, lived in wooden buildings. Carved cedar totem poles indicated who lived in each house.

BARK SHELTER
Some tribes built huts from chunks of redwood or cedar bark. The sweet-smelling wood repelled insects.

Discover more in Tepees

Tepees

The Plains Indians lived in cone-shaped structures called tepees, made out of buffalo hides sewn together. When tribes needed to move on to find food or to escape from enemies, they could fold the tepees and transport them easily. At first, they carried their belongings on dog travois, so tepees were limited in size to the height of a man. Later, when horses were used for transportation, the tepees became much bigger. The space inside these portable homes was very limited, and the furniture was simple and functional. Buffalo skins made comfortable bedding. Backrests of willow rods laced together with string and supported by poles formed chairs, which could be rolled up neatly. Rawhide saddlebags called "parfleches" doubled as cushions or pillows. Tepees were erected with the steeper, rear side against the westerly winds, and the doorway facing east, towards the rising sun. In the windy areas of the southern plains, the Sioux and Cheyenne supported their tepees with three foundation poles, while further north, the Hidatsa, Crow and Blackfeet used four poles. Ceremonial and larger tepees had more supports.

TEPEE DECORATION
Ornaments were tied to the top of the tepee poles. These are leather thongs wrapped in grass and tipped with yarn tufts.

Family possessions
Families kept everything they owned inside their tepee. It was kitchen, bedroom, playroom, living room and shed all in the one space.

Symbols of the Blackfeet
Painted symbols, such as rainbow stripes or a buffalo head, protected the tepee owners against sickness and bad luck.

RESERVATION CAMP
When the Plains Indians were forced to move to reservations by the United States government, they took their tepees with them and pitched them in tribal groups. They tried to preserve as much of the way of life from their homelands as possible.

Smoke flaps
These could be opened from the inside with a pair of long poles.

TEPEE CAMPS

Tepee camps were pitched in a C shape with the opening facing east. Behavior inside the tepee followed strict rules. An open door was a sign of welcome. Men entered to the right, women to the left. Younger men remained silent until they were invited to speak. No one walked between the fire and another person. Visitors brought their own bowls, and when the host cleaned his pipe, it was time for visitors to leave.

N

Dew cloth
A decorated lining called a dew cloth was tied inside the tepee. It kept out moisture and helped to insulate the tepee.

BUFFALO SKIN
Hides were tanned and smoked so that they would be waterproof but still remain soft. Some were decorated for ceremonial tepees or painted with a family clan's symbol.

Lacing
The tepee was laced from the bottom to the smoke hole with pins carved from flexible willow wood.

Entrance
The door was made from a flap of skin and was oval or V-shaped.

Fireplace
The fire was placed under the smoke hole, and the woodpile was near the door.

Hemline
The hem was pegged to the ground with stakes but raised in hot weather to let in air.

COMPACT CARVING
Totem pole carvers used pictures to tell stories. They compressed images of symbolic creatures, such as those shown here, into small spaces.

SUN MASK
This Bella Coola mask was worn during winter ceremonies. The central symbol represents the spirit of the life-giving sun.

THUNDERBIRD MASK
Kwakiutl masks sometimes had movable parts. When the pieces of this bird's beak swing open, they reveal a human mask.

• CEREMONIES AND RITUALS •

Totems, Masks and Kachinas

On the Northwest Coast, woodcarvers turned cedar trees into totem poles to record the history of a family or an important person. Figures of animals, such as Sea Grizzly Bear, and mythical creatures, such as Thunderbird, told of clans' connections with their spirit ancestors. These characters were easily recognized. Raven clan's symbol was a bird's head with a straight beak; Eagle clan's emblem had a beak that curved. Totem artists also carved masks for storytelling and rituals. The wearers took on the power of the spirits that the masks represented. Tribes in other regions used masks, too. The Southwest Hopis had dozens of kachina masks. In the Northeast, the Iroquoian False Face Society wore elaborate wood and horsehair masks and the Husk Face Society whispered fortunes through cornhusk masks.

KACHINA DOLLS

Southwestern tribes, such as the Zuni and the Hopi, carved kachina dolls out of wood. They clothed them in masks and costumes to look exactly like the men who dressed up as kachina spirits. These dolls were not playthings. They were given to the children to teach them to identify the many different kachinas and the parts they played in tribal ceremonies.

Zuni kachina doll

TODAY'S TOTEM ART
Thunderbird, on top of this modern totem, is the carver's personal crest and shows he belongs to a Kwakiutl warrior group.

DOGFISH MASK
A dancer wearing this dogfish mask pulled a string to make the figure riding the dorsal fin twirl.

SEA OTTER MASK
The curved arms around the sea otter's head whirl around and support birds with flapping cloth wings.

201

Special Occasions

Native Americans enjoyed many special occasions. They celebrated important times in people's lives, such as reaching the age of puberty, getting married or being successful in battle. Ceremonial clothing, decorated with fur, feathers, quilling and beadwork, was worn for these events, and people made necklaces, earrings and bracelets from animal teeth, bones and claws, shells and stones. Native Americans believed that the sky, the soil, plants, birds, animals, rivers and everything else had spirits that must be respected. These spirits could be reached through dance, song, prayer and other religious rituals. Some tribes also worshipped monsters, such as the dreadful Cannibal Spirit of the Northwest, and danced to show their evil power.

SACRED ROOM
The underground "kiva" was the holy place of Southwest kachina priests. The chamber's floor became an altar when it was sprinkled with cornmeal, sand, ground bark and flowers.

DRESSED TO DANCE
Kwakiutl shamans wore cedar bark costumes and painted wooden masks to represent the birdlike friends of the fearsome Cannibal Spirit.

CANNIBAL SPIRIT DANCERS
The Cannibal Spirit dancer is standing on the left wearing a cedar bark ring around his neck. His fearsome followers squat in front.

FAMILY JEWELRY
Navajo women wore ear pendants before marriage. Afterwards, they attached them to bead necklaces until their own daughters were old enough to wear them.

FEATHER HEADDRESS
Ceremonial costumes made from eagle feathers, like this chieftain's war bonnet, had special importance. Eagles were linked with heavenly spirits and admired for their speed, fierceness and sharp eyesight.

POLLEN RITUAL
A blessing of pollen, the tribe's most powerful "medicine," is a highlight of the four-day puberty ritual for an Apache girl. Baskets of yellow pollen from tule rushes are gathered for the ceremony. The grains are then sprinkled over the girl's hair and face.

Pollen basket

Discover more in Pipes and Powwows

SNOWSHOE DANCER
An Objibwa hunter rejoices after the first winter snowfall. Now his prey will flounder in drifts and be much easier to catch.

FLUTED MELODY
Flute music, called the "wind that breathes life into the heart," accompanied many dances. The six round holes represented the Earth, sky and the four directions: north, south, east and west.

MARKING TIME
This rattle has a dried gourd body, a handle covered in glass beads and streamers made from feathers and strips of sinew.

• CEREMONIES AND RITUALS •

Ceremonial Dancing

Ceremonial dancing was the Native American way of celebrating joyous occasions and praying for health, successful hunting and good harvests. Plains Sioux imitated the sounds and movements of bears before the hunt or whooped in a scalp dance after a battle victory. The Californian Patwin tribe danced in huge headdresses and cloaks made of feathers or grass to encourage the growth of wild crops. Hopi men in the dry Southwest collected snakes for an elaborate ritual. The snake priests, wearing feathered headdresses and kilts patterned with the serpent motif, circled the village square with the reptiles in their mouths. Their companions stroked the creatures with eagle feathers to stop them from biting. The snakes were then returned to the desert where their lightning-like, zigzag movements were supposed to bring pre-harvest rain.

KACHINA SPIRITS

Hopi men impersonated kachinas, important spirits in their religion. They performed dances during the seasons of seed sowing, plant growth and harvesting. Kachina dancers taught young children tribal ways and gave them dolls.

Kachina doll

RATTLING RHYTHM
Inuit (Eskimo) men wore sealskin gauntlet gloves for ceremonial dancing. This pair is decorated with horned puffin beaks and quills from feathers, which rattled to the beat of the drum.

TAPPING RHYTHM
An Inuit (Eskimo) woodcarver made this baton. The woodpecker is attached to the shaft with springy whale cartilage. During the dance, it pecks like a real bird.

205

Pipes and Powwows

Native Americans used solemn pipe-smoking rituals to ask for the spirits' help to make war, peace or rain, to hunt successfully, or to seal a good trade bargain. Pipes were very special and very beautiful. Each one took several weeks to make. The stem was hollow wood, and the bowl was fashioned from soft soapstone, clay or wood. Supernatural powers did not flow through the pipe until these two parts were ceremonially joined. In the past, pipes were smoked at powwows where people gathered to pray for the sick or for the tribe's success in battle or hunting. Today, powwows are joyful events, held at least once a year, to remind people of old customs and to celebrate new ones.

TOBACCO BAG
The pipe bowl, the pipe stem and the smoking mixture were kept in a quilled and beaded buckskin pouch.

PIPE CEREMONY
Ceremonial pipe smoking had special importance. As one Sioux tribesman explained: "This pipe is us. The stem is our backbone, the bowl our head. The stone is our blood, red as our skin."

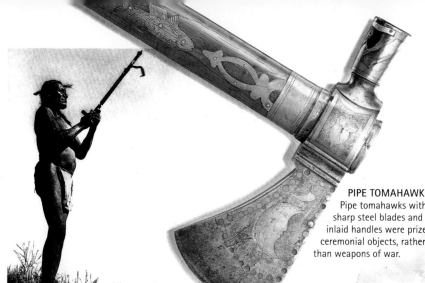

PIPE TOMAHAWK
Pipe tomahawks with sharp steel blades and inlaid handles were prized ceremonial objects, rather than weapons of war.

IVORY PIPE
Arctic pipes were often made of ivory. This one was carved from the tusk of an Arctic walrus.

PRAYER RITUAL
A Sioux warrior placed a buffalo skull at his feet and pointed his pipe skyward while he prayed for supernatural powers.

TOBACCO PLANT
Tobacco was believed to have magical powers to heal or to hurt, to change people's fortunes, or to call up good spirits and drive away evil.

THE POWWOW CIRCUITS

The original powwows were meetings of Plains Indians. Now these celebrations of Indian life and tradition are held in Canada and the United States, from the Pacific Northwest to the Atlantic. In cities, the venue is a large gymnasium or open park. In the country, powwow organizers set up special grounds. Performers of traditional dances spend the summer months traveling the powwow circuit. These cheerful, colorful festivities also involve singers, craftspeople, families, friends and the local community.

Northwest drum

Healers and Healing

Calling a doctor was no simple matter for Native Americans. Often, visits and ceremonial treatments lasted for several days. They were organized by healers, known as shamans or medicine men and women, some of whom had as much power as any chief. Shamans cured the sick with herbs, performed healing rituals, told the future or found missing property. They knew the dances, chants, prayers and ceremonies that would bring good fortune to their tribes and please the spirits. Young people had to take many difficult tests of physical strength before they could become shamans, and few succeeded. They did not receive their special powers until they had seen a vision in the form of a sacred animal or object. Native Americans were generally very healthy until fatal diseases were introduced from Europe.

MEDICINE KIT
A Sioux woman once owned this rawhide bag of medicines. The wrapped bundles contained crushed leaves and powdered bark and roots.

SWEAT LODGES
Skins over a wooden frame made an airtight hut. Inside, water poured on hot stones turned to steam, like a modern sauna. Warriors cleansed their bodies and the sick eased fevers and aching bones.

PRAYER SNAKES
Some tribes thought that snakes caused stomach complaints. To cure such gastric upsets, Navajo medicine men made snake-shaped prayer sticks from wood and feathers.

DRY SAND PAINTING
Navajo healers used powdered rocks to create large pictures on the floor of the patient's dwelling. They believed the sand could absorb evil sickness. After the ritual, they destroyed the painting.

TOOL OF TRADE
Rattles were an essential part of the Tlingit shaman's ritual equipment. This one's wild hair, beard and mustache are made from human hair.

HONORED HEALER
Slow Bull, photographed on the Plains with a sacred buffalo skull, was a well-respected Oglala Sioux medicine man.

HERBS AND FLOWERS
Native Americans used many herbal medicines. From willow bark they extracted a pain-relieving ingredient, used in today's aspirin. Southeastern Cherokees believed every plant would cure a specific sickness. Iris roots ground with suet, lard and beeswax made an ointment for cuts and grazes. Juice of lady's slipper roots eased pain, soothed hysterics and relieved colds and flu.

Wild purple iris

Yellow lady's slipper

209

FOE KILLED
The Sioux clipped and dyed feathers to count special coups. A red spot indicated the wearer had killed his foe.

SINGLE WOUND
A feather dyed red meant the wearer had been wounded in battle.

MANY COUPS
A jagged edge proclaimed that the wearer had felled several enemies.

MANY WOUNDS
Split feathers were a sign that the wearer had been wounded many times.

FOE SCALPED
A notched feather showed the wearer had cut his enemy's throat and then taken his scalp.

THROAT CUT
The top of the feather clipped diagonally signaled that the wearer had cut his foe's throat without scalping him.

GREAT WARRIOR
Braves who fought well became respected war leaders and were entitled to wear elaborate ceremonial costumes.

• A CHANGING WORLD •

Warriors and Warfare

Some Native American tribes hated war, but many fought constantly over land and horses, to avenge their people and to rack up battle honors. They carried out hit-and-run raids more often than full-scale warfare. Sometimes they adopted prisoners; other times they tortured or scalped them. Southeastern men wore loincloths and moccasins on the warpath and carried weapons and moccasin repair kits. The men walked in single file, and stepped in the footprints of the warrior in front. Chickasaw scouts tied bear paws to their feet to lay confusing trails. Northeasterners stalked the woodlands, signaling to each other with animal calls, or clashed in canoes on the Great Lakes. Plains warriors considered hand-to-hand fighting more courageous and skillful than firing arrows from a distance. A brave proclaimed his "coup" (French for "blow") score by attaching golden eagle tail feathers to his war bonnet and ceremonial robe.

WAR SHIELDS
Warriors prized their buffalo hide shields. Some were covered with deerskin and decorated with symbolic animals, bells and feathers.

TROPHIES OF WAR

In some tribes, scalps brought honor to the warrior who took them. In others, counting coups or capturing horses from the enemy were much more important. Native Americans believed the scalp contained a person's soul and that spiritual power flowed from the slain warrior to the victorious brave. After a successful battle, many tribes danced through the night around the scalps of their foes. They preserved these war trophies by stretching them over a wooden hoop attached to a stick.

WAR WHISTLE
When a Mandan warrior saw an enemy, he blew a whistle like this, which is made from bone wrapped in porcupine quills.

BOWS AND ARROWS
Warriors carried their tightly strung bows and sharp arrows in tanned leather cases.

Arrival of Strangers

In 1492, Caribbean islanders saw Columbus's ships approaching. They thought they came from the sky, home of powerful spirits. Columbus inspired adventurous Europeans from the "Old World" to visit America, the "New World." People from Spain, England, France and Russia came in search of land, minerals and furs. Some tried to convert the tribes to their religion; others used them as slaves. Europe acquired trade goods and new foods, such as chocolate, sunflowers, corn and peanuts; Native Americans gained guns, horses, metal tools and whiskey. Old and New worlds did not mix well. White settlers often took land by force and shot thousands of buffalo for sport. Native Americans, who shared most things and wasted little, could not understand this behavior. One old man despaired, "When the buffalo went away, the hearts of my people fell to the ground, and they could not lift them up again."

CHRISTIAN MISSIONARIES
The Spanish brought Christianity and hard labor to the Southeast, Southwest and California. Many Native Americans died from new diseases and harsh treatment.

212

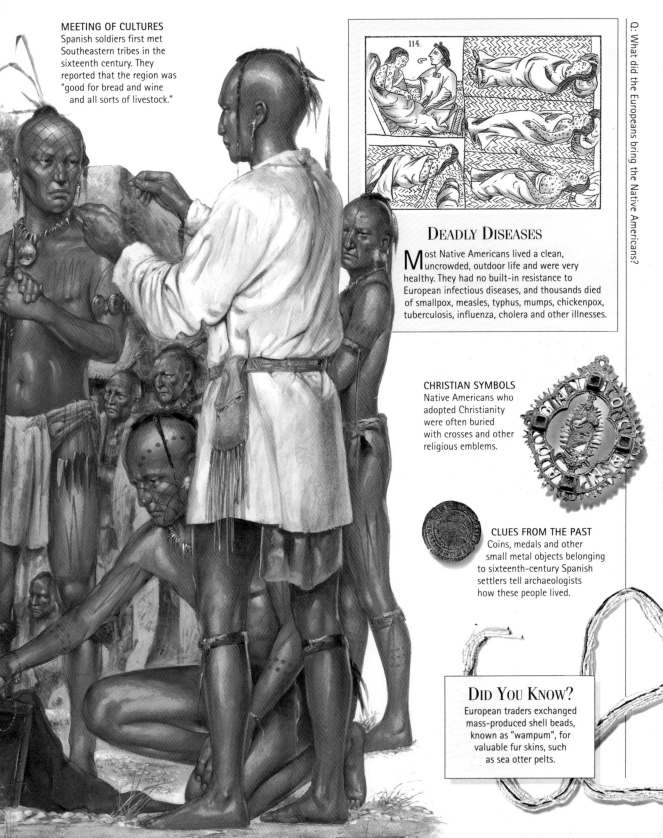

MEETING OF CULTURES
Spanish soldiers first met Southeastern tribes in the sixteenth century. They reported that the region was "good for bread and wine and all sorts of livestock."

DEADLY DISEASES

Most Native Americans lived a clean, uncrowded, outdoor life and were very healthy. They had no built-in resistance to European infectious diseases, and thousands died of smallpox, measles, typhus, mumps, chickenpox, tuberculosis, influenza, cholera and other illnesses.

CHRISTIAN SYMBOLS
Native Americans who adopted Christianity were often buried with crosses and other religious emblems.

CLUES FROM THE PAST
Coins, medals and other small metal objects belonging to sixteenth-century Spanish settlers tell archaeologists how these people lived.

DID YOU KNOW?
European traders exchanged mass-produced shell beads, known as "wampum", for valuable fur skins, such as sea otter pelts.

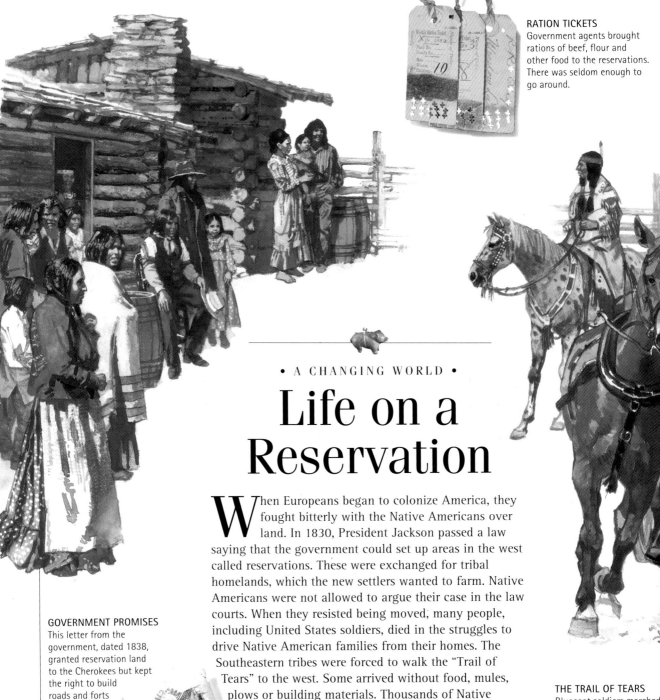

RATION TICKETS
Government agents brought rations of beef, flour and other food to the reservations. There was seldom enough to go around.

• A CHANGING WORLD •

Life on a Reservation

When Europeans began to colonize America, they fought bitterly with the Native Americans over land. In 1830, President Jackson passed a law saying that the government could set up areas in the west called reservations. These were exchanged for tribal homelands, which the new settlers wanted to farm. Native Americans were not allowed to argue their case in the law courts. When they resisted being moved, many people, including United States soldiers, died in the struggles to drive Native American families from their homes. The Southeastern tribes were forced to walk the "Trail of Tears" to the west. Some arrived without food, mules, plows or building materials. Thousands of Native Americans perished from hunger and misery. Although reservation schools taught the ways of white people, Native Americans never forgot where they had come from, and children learned their own customs from their parents and grandparents.

GOVERNMENT PROMISES
This letter from the government, dated 1838, granted reservation land to the Cherokees but kept the right to build roads and forts within the area.

THE TRAIL OF TEARS
Bluecoat soldiers marched 16,000 Cherokees along "the trail where they cried." Two thousand died along the way, and another 2,000 died soon after the long journey.

214

RESERVATION LANDS

The dark color marks the reservations set up by the United States government in the west. These small areas often had poor soil and a bad climate. Native Americans were expected to grow their own food, and this caused great hardship because many tribes had never farmed before. They were unable to hunt or to move around freely any more, and their new life often made them feel like prisoners.

COLORING CRAYONS
Some Native Americans who ran reservation stores could not write. They used crayons to draw pictures of what they sold.

SEWING LESSONS
In the reservation schools, children wore uniforms and were taught to read and write English. The girls used sewing machines to make European-style clothing.

215

COILED CLAY
Zuni craftspeople still use the traditional coil method for making pots out of local clays. They apply paints mixed from minerals with a chewed yucca leaf brush.

MICKEY MOCCASINS
Beadwork is a very old Native American craft. The designs of some moccasins now show modern influences.

Arts and Crafts

Native Americans made practical and beautifully crafted objects for everyday use. Their ceremonial clothing and sacred things were richly decorated. Painting, carving and embroidery told stories and were linked with the spirits through designs that had special meanings. Skills such as basketry, pottery and weaving have been passed down from one generation to another for many centuries. The Navajo learned silversmithing from the Mexicans in the 1850s, and then taught the Hopi and Zuni. Today, many artists and craftspeople use modern materials and tools. They take ideas from the twentieth century and blend them with patterns from the past, often using vibrant colors in their work. Native American arts and crafts are now famous throughout the world.

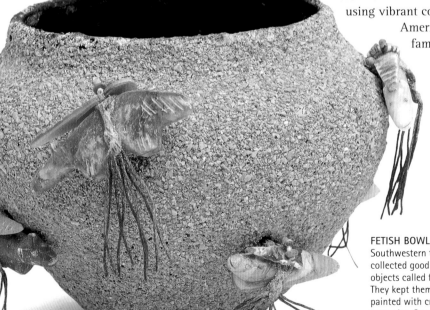

HANDCRAFTED JEWELRY
Turquoise, mined by Southwestern tribes, is the stone of happiness, health and good fortune.

FETISH BOWL
Southwestern tribes collected good luck objects called fetishes. They kept them in bowls painted with crushed turquoise. Some fetishes were strapped to the outside.

216

MINIATURE KACHINA
Some Zuni and Hopi artists make kachina dolls to sell. This one wears a mask topped with a feather plume and carries a rattle in its right hand.

PIECES OF SILVER
Navajo jewelers often make belts from sterling silver. This one has oval shell shapes alternating with butterfly spacers and is set with natural green turquoise stones.

CLAY FIGURE
"Uncle Fidel's Cousin San Luis" was sculptured by a Pueblo potter, Nora Naranjo-Morse. When Nora has her hands on clay, she feels she has "come home."

DID YOU KNOW?
The Zuni believed that the spirits of animals and plants lived in objects that looked like them. Traditional animal fetishes were usually naturally shaped stones. Modern ones may be carved.

Discover more in Totems, Masks and Kachinas

Glossary

Rosemary

Mycenaean fresco

Miniature wine jug

Voting tokens

Terra-cotta statue

acropolis Meaning "high city." In Mycenaean times most of a city was on high ground. Later, Greeks placed temples, shrines, and other important buildings on hills above their cities.

acupuncture A Chinese treatment for illness, first practiced in ancient times. It involves inserting needles under the skin at certain points on the body.

AD An abbreviation for the Latin "anno Domini," meaning "in the year of our Lord." Used for the measurement of time, AD indicates the number of years since the supposed date of Christ's birth.

agora The open space in the middle of a Greek city used for meetings and markets.

amphitheater An oval arena, surrounded by a seating area, for mass entertainment.

amulet A charm or piece of jewelry worn as protection against evil.

ancestor A member of your family who died a long time ago.

ankh A symbol that meant life. It was carried by gods and pharaohs. Later, the ankh was adopted as a Christian symbol.

anonymous Without a name. The work of individual artisans in ancient China was not acknowledged by name.

archaeologist A person who studies the way people in the past lived by analysing the things they left behind, such as tomb goods, tools, weapons, and cooking pots.

architecture The art of planning, designing, and constructing buildings.

assembly The main governing body of a democratic city-state. All citizens had the right to attend the assembly.

Ba An Egyptian word for a person's spirit, similar to the word "soul".

barbarians The ancient Chinese name for the people who lived beyond China's borders and did not share its customs. It was also a term used by the Greeks and Romans to describe foreigners.

bartering A system of trade by which goods of the same value are exchanged, and money is not used.

basilica An ancient Roman building that contained government offices and law courts.

BC Before Christ. Used for the measurement of time, BC indicates the number of years before the supposed date of Christ's birth.

Black Land The fertile soil in the River Nile valley and delta. The Egyptians called this land "kemet."

black–figure ware A style of decorating pottery that featured black figures on a red background.

bronze A combination of copper and tin, and sometimes lead.

Bronze Age The period of time when a civilization first discovered how to make bronze and then used it for tools, weapons, and other things.

bullboat Circular craft made from a framework of willow branches covered with buffalo hide.

Byzantine Empire The Eastern Roman Empire from the time of Constantine I until the fall of Constantinople in 1453.

c. An abbreviation of circa, which means "about." Used with dates to mean "at the approximate time of."

calligraphy The art of writing with a brush dipped in ink. Faultless writing looked natural and "alive" with strong strokes, invisible joins, and even-textured ink.

camphor A sharp-smelling substance taken from camphor trees. The ancient Chinese used it to flavor sweet dishes.

canal An artificial waterway. Canals in ancient China were dug by hand.

canopic jars Small jars for storing the organs of a dead person when the body was mummified.

cartonnage A material made from scraps of linen or papyrus glued together with plaster or resin. Cartonnage was often used for mummy cases.

cattail A tall marsh plant with reedlike leaves. Many Native Americans ate its pollen and roots.

cavalry A unit of soldiers on horseback.

century A period of time lasting 100 years. It also refers to a unit of the Roman army, originally containing 100 men, but later reduced to 80 men.

ceramics Articles produced from clay and other substances that have been fired in a kiln.

charcoal The carbon remains of burnt materials. It was used as an ingredient in gunpowder.

citizen In ancient Greece, a freeborn man entitled to take part in the government of his city-state. In ancient Rome, a citizen was originally a freeborn man from Italy. Later, all freeborn men who lived in the Roman world could become citizens.

civilization An organized society that has developed social customs, government, technology, and the arts.

clan A group of people related to each other by ancestry or marriage.

colonnade A set of evenly spaced columns that often supports a roof.

Coyote The mischievous wolf spirit that loved playing tricks.

creation stories Different stories told by Native Americans to explain where they came from.

cremate To burn a dead body.

crook A stick with a curved top carried by a god or pharaoh to symbolize kingship.

democracy In ancient Greece, a system of government in which all citizens could have a say.

demotic script A form of ancient Egyptian writing that developed from hieratic script from 700 BC onwards. It was used for administration and business.

dragon A mythical creature. The ancient Chinese worshiped the spirits of dragons. The five-toed dragon became the First Emperor's special symbol.

dyke A barrier to stop water flooding. The ancient Chinese tried to control a flooding river by building a dyke. They drove stakes into the banks and piled bundles of sticks against them.

dynasty A ruling family. Members of a dynasty were related by birth, marriage, or adoption.

Egyptologist A special kind of archaeologist who finds out about how people lived in ancient Egypt by studying the things they left behind.

embalmer A person who treats a dead body with spices and oils to prevent it decaying.

emblem A decorative mark or symbol that means something special.

Eskimos (see also Inuit) Dwellers in the Arctic region. Eskimo means "eaters of raw meat," but they cooked at least part of their daily ration.

excavate To uncover an object, a skeleton, or even a whole town by digging.

flax A plant from which thread can be made and woven into linen.

freedman/freedwoman A man or woman who has been freed from slavery.

fresco A painting made with watercolors on wet plaster.

frieze A strip of painting or carving on a temple or a tomb wall that told a story.

garlic A herb used by the ancient Chinese to treat colds, whooping cough, and other illnesses.

gild To cover in gold leaf.

gladiator A man, or sometimes a woman, trained to fight in public to provide entertainment.

glaze A shiny coating that gives a smooth, glossy surface. Glaze is usually applied to pottery or porcelain, but other materials can also be glazed.

gold leaf A very thin sheet of beaten gold.

hemp A plant with tough fibers that can be woven into fabric and rope.

Herodotus (c.485–c.425 BC) A Greek writer and traveler who is regarded as the father of history. He lived from about 485 BC to 425 BC. He based his reports of the Persian Wars on eyewitness accounts and facts.

Hesiod (8th century BC) One of ancient Greece's earliest poets. He owned a farm in Boeotia.

hieratic script A faster form of writing than hieroglyphs. It was always written from right to left, unlike European languages, which are written from left to right.

hieroglyphs The symbols and pictures of ancient Egyptian writing.

Homer (8th century BC) A Greek poet who recited his long story poems, which were called epics. Little is known about him except that he may have been blind.

husky A breed of dog. They were the Inuits' (Eskimos') only domestic animal.

Hyksos people Foreigners, probably from Palestine or Syria, who invaded Egypt.

Ice Age A time when large parts of the Earth were covered with glaciers.

igloo A temporary winter dwelling built by some Arctic tribes from hard-packed snow.

Iliad Homer's long story poem about the war between the Greeks and the Trojans.

Tutankhamun's gold funeral mask

Hair comb and toys

Pyramids at Giza

Rosetta Stone

219

Crocodile mummy

Thunderbird mask

Inuit grass socks

incense An aromatic substance extracted from resin. Incense was used in ritual ceremonies.

infantry A unit of foot soldiers.

inlay A form of decoration in which one material is inserted into prepared slots or cavities in the surface of another material to form a pattern or a picture.

Inuit (see also Eskimos) Many tribes in the Arctic prefer to be known as Inuit. This is their word for "people."

irrigation The process of supplying water to the land using canals or ditches.

jade An extremely hard mineral. The jade in ancient China was nephrite, a white stone streaked with reds or browns. The more familiar green jadeite was not known in China until much later.

junk A Chinese sailing boat. Chinese boat builders stiffened the sails with bamboo rods.

Ka An Egyptian word for a person's life force created at birth and released by death.

kachinas Supernatural spirits who guided the tribes of the Southwest of America.

kiva A Native American place of worship and a council chamber, usually built below ground.

lacquer A natural plastic varnish that resists heat, moisture, acids, alkalis, and bacteria, and is made from the milky sap of the lacquer tree.

legion A unit of the Roman army. It varied in size throughout the history of the Empire.

linear Made up of lines. The linear designs on Stone Age (Neolithic) pottery were made with a soft brush.

Linear A An early form of writing used by the ancient Minoans.

Linear B A form of writing that the Mycenaeans adapted from Linear A.

loincloth Cloth or skin draped between the legs and looped through a belt. Worn by many Native Americans living in a warm climate.

loom A wooden frame used to hold the threads during the process of weaving.

magistrate A government official who judged the local criminals and looked after the affairs of a district or province.

medicine man/woman A shaman with special powers to heal and contact the spirits.

Rawhide playing cards

Inuit sunglasses

Saddle bag

migrating When people or animals move from one country or place to another.

minister A high-ranking government official who advised the Chinese emperor and helped to see that imperial laws were obeyed.

mosaic A pattern or a picture made from tiny pieces of colored stone, glass, or glazed earthenware set in a bed of soft mortar.

mummification A process of drying and embalming that preserves the dead body of a person or an animal.

mythology Stories passed down by word of mouth from one generation to another.

Neolithic A period of time when humans made tools and weapons of flint and stone. Neolithic is the final stage of the Stone Age.

New World A name used by the Europeans for the land area that included Canada, North America, and South America.

nomads People who move continually from place to place to find food for themselves and pasture for their animals.

nomarch An official in charge of a province or region called a nome. There were 42 nomes in ancient Egypt.

oasis (singular), oases (plural) A fertile patch in the desert with its own water supply.

Odyssey Homer's long story poem about the adventures of the Greek hero Odysseus.

Old World The part of the world that was known by Europeans before the discovery of the Americas. It included Europe, Asia, and Africa.

omen A sign or warning about the future that indicated a happy or disastrous event.

oracle A message spoken by a priest or priestess on behalf of a god.

order A style of architecture. The three Greek orders were Doric, Ionic, and Corinthian.

palette A flat piece of wood or stone on which artists mixed paints.

papyrus A reed that the ancient Egyptians made into paper and other objects.

parfleche A saddlebag made from rawhide in the pattern of an envelope. From the French "parer une flèche," meaning "to turn an arrow."

patricians Aristocratic members of Roman society who held important positions in government.

pharaoh The ruler of ancient Egypt. The name comes from the ancient Egyptian word "per-ao," meaning "the great house." It referred to the palace where the pharaoh lived.

philosopher A person who searches for knowledge and wisdom. Ancient Greek philosophers studied the natural world and human behavior. Some of their writings survive.

Plato (c.427–c.347 BC) An Athenian philosopher. Plato's ideas for running an ideal state are still studied today.

plebeians Common, low-born members of Roman society. The plebeians were the poorest and most numerous class of Roman citizens.

porcelain A thin china made from fine kaolin clay that was found in the Chinese mountains.

porcupine An animal covered with long protective quills. Native American women softened and dyed the quills and used them for embroidery.

province Any area outside the city of Rome (later outside Italy) that was controlled by the Romans.

qilin A mythical animal also called a Chinese unicorn. It symbolized long life, greatness, happiness, and wise government.

Red Land The desert that lay beyond the Nile River valley and delta. The ancient Egyptians called this land "deshret."

red-figure ware A style of decorating pottery that featured red figures on a black background.

relief A picture carved into a flat slab of stone.

republic A form of government in which the people elect representatives.

resin A thick, waterproof, sticky substance obtained from some plants and trees.

ritual The pattern of behavior for a ceremonial dance or religious ceremony.

Rosetta Stone An inscribed slab of granite that gave the major clue to deciphering hieroglyphs. It was found by a French soldier near the village of Rosetta, in Egypt, in 1799. The stone is 3 ft 7 in (114 cm) high, 2 ft 3 in (72 cm) wide, 11 in (28 cm) thick, and weighs 1,684 pounds (762 kg). The Rosetta Stone is now in London's British Museum.

rudder A flat piece of wood attached to the stern of a boat below the waterline, which is used for steering. The rudder was a Chinese invention.

sacred object Something used in a religious ceremony, for example, a buffalo's skull.

sarcophagus (singular), sarcophagi (plural) A large stone box that enclosed a coffin. The surfaces were usually carved in relief.

shaman A medicine man or woman with special powers to heal and contact the spirits.

shrine A place where the ancient Greeks and Romans worshiped one of their gods.

soothsayer A person who predicts the future.

sphinx A mythical creature usually depicted with the head of a woman and the body of a lion.

Stone Age The time when humans made tools and weapons from stone.

stylus A writing tool. The pointed end was used to mark the covering of wax on a wooden tablet.

supernatural Relating to things belonging to the world of the spirits.

sweat lodge An airtight hut filled with steam—the Native American equivalent of a sauna.

symbol A decorative mark in a painting or carving that means something special.

terra-cotta Unglazed, reddish-brown clay that was used to make roof tiles and to model small statues. The ancient Chinese made terracotta models and figures to be placed in tombs.

trance A hypnotic state resembling sleep. At Greek shrines, priests and priestesses often fell into a trance before speaking oracles.

trireme A Greek warship with three rows of oars.

tundra A treeless area with permanently frozen subsoil that lies between the ice of the Arctic and the timber line of North America and Eurasia.

vision A religious experience that brought a person into contact with the spirits.

vizier Chief adviser to the pharaoh and second only to him in importance.

wickiup A dwelling used in the Southwest of America made of poles covered with branches.

wigwam A shelter used by tribes in the Northeast and Great Lakes areas of North America. They bent four saplings towards a center and covered them with long strips of bark sewn together.

woolly mammoth A large hairy animal that became extinct at the end of the Ice Age. It had a trunk like an elephant and curved tusks.

Bronze and turquoise bird

Han bronze seal

Tang pottery dancer

Tang pottery camel

Index

Abu Simbel, 8, 28, 29
Abydos, 10
Achilles, 122
Acropolis, 90, 94, 95, 109, 118
actors, 155
acupuncture, 78–9
Aeschines, 96
afterlife, 20–1, 24–5
Agamemnon, King, 90
Age of Pyramids, 10
agoras, 108–9, 116
agriculture, 8, 12, 32–3, 54, 70–1, 90, 92, 94, 106, 110, 132, 146, 147, 164, 174
Ahmose, 11, 48
Akhenaten, 12, 45
Alaric, King, 166
alchemists, 58, 79, 84
Alexander the Great, 8, 11, 50, 51, 104, 122, 123, 124, 126
Alexandria, 8, 51, 124–5
alphabet, 102–3
Amarna, 8, 12, 45
Amenophis III, 28
Ammit, 24
amphitheaters, 144, 154
amulets, 22, 23, 24, 40–1
ancestor worship, 57, 64, 66, 73
animals, 91, 98, 106, 109, 112, 114
    family life, and, 34
    gods depicted as, 16–17
    hunting, 30
    mummies, 25
    skins, 176, 177, 178, 184, 198, 199
    symbols, 78
Antigonas, 124
Anubis, 17, 22, 23, 24
Apache people, 178, 186, 203
Aphrodite, 90, 98, 99, 124
Apollo, 93, 98, 99, 103, 118
aqueducts, 144
Arabs, 50
archaeology, 98, 132, 172
Archaic Period, 10, 89
architecture, 100–1, 118–19, 126
Ares, 98
Arissteides, 97
armed forces, 95, 102, 106, 120–3, 132, 150, 156, 158–9, 161, 164
armor, 90, 120, 121, 123, 154, 158
Artemis, 99, 101
artisans, 56, 62, 63, 66, 68, 82–3
arts and crafts, 55–7, 62, 72, 82–3, 89, 110–1, 116–19, 124, 126, 132–3, 148–9, 160, 162, 178, 189, 216–17
Asclepius, 114
Asia Minor, 90, 92, 109, 124
assemblies, 96–7
Assyrians, 11, 50, 51
Aswan Dam, 29
Aten, 45
Athena, 94, 98, 118, 124
Athens, 94, 95, 96, 97, 108–9, 115, 116, 118, 120, 126, 127
athletics, 102, 112–13, 114
Attila the Hun, 164–5
augurs, 132, 136
Augustus, 51, 134, 158, 160, 161

Ba, 20–1
Bacchus, 136, 141, 160
Banpo, 55
barbarians, 164, 165, 166–7
bartering, 14–15, 42
basilicas, 144
baskets, 186, 191
Bastet, 16, 47

bathhouses, 150–1
Bering Strait, 172, 173
berries, 190, 191
Bes, 16, 41
black-figure ware, 117
Black Land, 8
Blackfoot people, 174, 198
boats, 11, 17, 30, 48
Book of the Dead, 21, 24, 44
books, 80, 82
bows and arrows, 178, 210, 211
boys, 102, 105
bridges, arched, 84
Britain, 130, 139, 146, 151, 160–1
bronze, 56–7, 82, 83, 88, 92, 116, 121, 132
Bronze Age, 88, 110
Bubastis, 43
Buddhism, 60, 62
buffalo, 174, 212
buildings, 100–1, 118–19, 124–5, 134–5, 144
bullboats, 185
Byzantine Empire, 164, 168–9
Byzantium, 127

Caesar, Julius, 51, 134
Cai Lun, 80
Cairo, 8
calligraphy, 80–1
camels, 63
cameos, 135, 148
camphor, 62
canals, 58, 60–1
Cannibal Spirit, 202, 203
canoes and kayaks, 184–5
canopic jars, 22
Caracalla, 150
card games, 172
caribou, 174, 177
cartouches, 12
CAT scanning, 21
catacombs, 162–3
cats, 9, 25, 34
cattle, 15
cavalry, 120, 122, 158
censors, 69
censuses, 164
centuries, 158, 159
centurions, 158
ceremonies, 178, 181, 200–9
Champollion, Jean-Francois, 39
Chang'an, 62–3
chariot races, 154
Cherokee people, 209
chess, 84
Cheyenne people, 194, 198
Chickasaw people, 210
chickees, 196
children and babies, 72, 76, 95, 100, 101, 102–3, 138, 140–1, 142, 150, 152, 178–9, 186, 194, 203
chili peppers, 194
chimaera, 132
Chinese parsley, 79
Chong Er, 76
chopsticks, 76
Christianity, 39, 50, 127, 136, 162–3, 167, 168, 169, 212, 213
circadian rhythm, 78
Circus Maximus, 154
citizenship, 96, 97, 106, 108, 120, 135, 138, 141, 142, 158
city life, 144–5
city-states, 94–5, 120
civil service, 60, 61, 68–9
civil war, 134, 164
class, 68–9, 74

Classical period, 89
Claudius, 135, 160
Cleopatra VII, 51, 124, 126
clothing, 36, 51, 62, 74–5, 100, 104–5, 121, 138, 141, 142–3, 152, 176–7, 178, 189, 202, 204, 210
coinage, 58, 92, 108, 109, 116, 124
Cold Food Day, 76
colonies, 92–3, 110, 124–7
colonization, 212–5
Colosseum, 154, 161
Columbus, Christopher, 212
columns, 118–19
Comanche people, 188
compasses, 84
Composite order, 119
Confucianism, 58, 60, 62, 68, 78
Constantine, 127, 163, 164, 165, 168–9
Constantinople, 127, 131, 164, 168–9
cooking, 194–5
copper, 74
Corinth, 94, 118
Corinthian order, 119, 127
corn, 174, 195
corn dole, 152, 165
Cossutius, 127
country life, 146–7
Coyote, 172, 187
cradleboards, 178, 179
craftspeople, 10, 14, 26, 42–3, 106, 108, 116–17, 148–9
creation stories, 172–3
Cree people, 175
cremation, 145
Crete, 88
crook, 13, 17
Crow people, 198
crowns, 13
Cush, 8
Cycladic civilization, 88, 89
Cyprus, 90

Dacia, 131, 160
dance, 18, 46, 47, 102, 106, 110–11, 202–3, 204–5
Daoism, 62, 79
Dark Age, 89, 92, 110
death, 127
Deir el-Bahri, 8
Delphi, 93
Demeter, 99
democracy, 96
demotic script, 39
Diocletian, 150, 164, 165
Dionysus, 136
disease, 213
diviners, 56, 57
doctors, 114–15, 150, 151
dog sleds, 186–7
Domitian, 134
Doric order, 118, 119
Dragon Boat Festival, 77
dragons, 54
drama, 112, 155
dry sand painting, 208–9
dynasties, 55, 56

eagles, 130, 158
Eastern Empire, 164, 166, 168–9
eating and drinking, 110–11
Edfu, 8, 50
Edict of Milan, 163
education, 38–9, 102–3, 126, 140–1
embalmers, 22–3
emperors, 64–5, 130, 134, 142, 152, 154, 160, 162
empire, 92–3, 110, 124–7

engineering, 132, 147
entertainment, 61, 63, 76, 77, 110–13, 124, 144, 154–5
equites, 135
Erechtheum, 118–19
Erlitou period, 55
Eros, 89
Etruscans, 132–3, 142, 148
European settlement, 212–4
exercise, 78, 79

family life, 27, 34–5, 72–3, 138
fasces, 134
feather symbols, 210
festivals, 16–17, 19, 46–7, 54, 72, 76–7, 112–13, 140, 141, 162
fetishes, 216, 217
fire brigades, 145
First Intermediate Period, 10
fish and fishing, 106, 110, 111, 192–3
Five Animal Exercises, 78
flax, 15, 32, 36
flooding, 8, 16–17, 32
food, 15, 32, 35, 62, 70, 76–7, 92, 106, 108, 109, 110–11, 146, 152–3, 190–5, 214
    afterlife, for the, 20, 25
    bartering, 42
    gods, for the, 18
footwear, 70, 74, 104, 108, 116, 177, 187, 216
foragers, 190–1
forum, 134–5
frescoes, 91, 146, 148
friezes, 118, 121, 148
furniture, 13, 34
Fustat, 50

gambling sticks, 183
games, 84, 178, 182–3
Gaozong, Emperor, 64
garlic, 79
Gaul, 130, 148, 160
gauntlet gloves, 205
Geometric period, 89, 116
ginseng, 79
girls, 100, 101, 102, 105
Giza, 8, 26, 27
gladiators, 154
glass, 149, 152
god-kings, 12–13
gods, 16–17, 18–19, 25, 28, 40, 45, 47, 90, 93, 94, 98–9, 102, 112, 114, 116, 126, 130, 132, 136–7, 146, 151, 162
gold, 10, 22–3, 26, 42, 63, 72, 74, 90, 92, 105, 116, 118, 142, 143, 152
government and law, 96–7, 124, 130, 134–5, 160
government officials, 60, 61, 68–9
grain, 152, 166
Grand Canal, 55, 61
grapes, 106–7, 110
grave robbers, 20, 50
Greek orders, 119
Guardians of the Hours, 79
gunpowder, 84

Hadrian, 143, 160
Hadrian's Wall, 130, 160–1
Hagia Sophia, 169
Haida people, 197
hair, 37, 178, 180, 181
Han dynasty, 55, 60–1, 83
Ha'py, 22
harbors, 156, 167
Haremhab, 12
harpoons, 192

harvesting, 15, 32
Hathor, 16, 18
Hatshepsut, Queen, 8, 12, 28
headdresses, 203
headwear, 74, 75
healers and healing, 172, 174, 208–9
health, 40–1, 114–15, 140, 150–1
heart, 24, 25, 40
Helen of Troy, 90
Hellenistic Age, 88, 89, 124–5
hemp, 70, 74
Hephaestus, 99, 116, 126
Hera, 99
Heracles, 122
herbs, 78, 79, 110, 114, 208, 209
Hermes, 98
Herodotus, 30, 121
Hesiod, 104
Hestia, 98
hetairai, 110–11
Hidatsa people, 198
hides, 176, 177, 178, 184, 198, 199
hieratic script, 38
hieroglyphs, 10, 30, 38–9
high priests, 11, 14, 19
Hippocrates, 114, 115
Homer, 91
homes, 100–1, 138, 144, 146, 196–9
hoop and pole, 183
Hopi people, 180, 181, 195, 200, 204, 205
hoplites, 120, 123
horses, 132, 154, 156, 188–9
Horus, 16, 17, 18, 40
hospitals, 150
houses, 34, 44, 68, 73
Hunefer, 24, 25
Huns, 164–5, 166
hunting, 9, 30, 31, 122, 172, 173, 174, 184, 190
Hupa people, 174
Husk Face Society, 200
huskies, 186–7
Hyksos, 11, 48

Ice Age, 172
igloos, 196
Imset, 22
incense, 18, 22–3
infantry, 158
Ingalik people, 193
Inhirkha, 34
Inuit people, 174, 176, 184, 192, 196, 205
inventions, 84–5
Ionic order, 119
iron, 60, 74, 82, 106, 116
Iroquoian False Face Society, 200
Iroquois people, 196
irrigation, 10, 14, 32, 33, 71
Isis, 16, 17, 20, 23, 28, 136
Islam, 50, 169
Isthmian Games, 112, 113
Italy, 90, 92, 124, 126–7, 131, 132, 146, 148, 160, 168
ivory, 90, 118

jade, 64, 72, 74, 82, 83
Janus, 132, 137
javelin throwing, 113
Jesus Christ, 162, 163
jewelry, 20, 36, 37, 41, 42, 49, 63, 74–5, 91, 104, 105, 116, 142, 143, 180, 181, 202, 203, 216, 217
Jews, 136
Jie Zhi Tui, 76
Justinian I, 168, 169

Ka, 20–1
kachinas, 200–1, 205, 217
Kalispel people, 174
Karnak, 8, 19, 28, 47
kayaks and canoes, 184–5
Khufu, 26

kickball, 182
Kimon, 97
kings, 130, 134
kinnikinnick, 207
kites, 85
kivas, 202
Kwakiutl people, 181, 200, 202

lacquerware, 72, 76, 82–3
lacrosse, 182
Lake Nasser, 29
Land of Two Kingdoms, 9
language, 168, 175, 189
Late Period, 10
Latin, 157, 168
laws, 58, 68
legions, 158, 159
Li Chun, 84
libraries, 150
life after death, 66
Linear B, 103
lions, 16, 27, 48
literature, 62
Liu Bang, 60
loincloth, 176
long boats, 184
longhouses, 196
looms, 100
lotus, 9, 30, 42, 43
Luxor, 8, 28, 47
Lydia, 109

Macedonia, 122–3, 124, 126
magistrates, 68–9
mammoths, 172
Mandan people, 175, 196
mandate of Heaven, 64
marble, 99, 116, 118, 121
Marcus Aurelius, 164
Mark Antony, 51
marketplace, 14–15
markets, 62–3
marriage, 100, 138–9, 180–1
masks, 172, 200–1
Maximian, 164
medicine, 78–9, 114–15, 151
medicine men/women, 174, 208–9
Medusa, 125
meeting places, 92, 108–9
Meketre, 15, 43
Memnon, Colossi of, 28
Memphis, 8
men, 100, 104, 105, 108, 111, 114, 120
Menelaus, 90
merchants, 62–3, 68, 106, 108, 144
metals, 42–3, 132, 143, 148
metate, 195
Middle Kingdom, 10, 54–5
migration, 92–3
ministers, 68
Minoan civilization, 89
Mithras, 136
moccasins, 177, 216
money, 15, 50, 58
mosaics, 146, 148–9, 152, 162, 167
Mount Olympus, 98–9
Mount Parnassus, 93
moxibustion, 78
mummies, 20, 21, 22–3, 23, 41
mummy case, 20–1, 24
Muses, 102, 103
music, 62, 67, 76, 102, 103, 106, 110, 112, 123, 132, 154
musical instruments, 204, 205
Mycenae, 88, 89, 90–1, 103
myths and legends, 54, 64, 70, 88, 90, 91, 98–9, 130, 132, 145, 172–3, 178, 187, 200–1, 202, 205

names, 72, 179
Naranjo-Morse, Nora, 217
Narmer, 9
natron, 22
Navajo people, 174, 203, 209, 217

navy, 120–1
Nefertiti, Queen, 12, 45
Nemean Games, 112, 113
Nero, 134
Netsilik people, 186
New Kingdom, 10
New Stone Age, 9
Nile River, 8, 12
nomarchs, 10, 14
nomes, 14, 49
Nootka people, 174
North Africa, 139, 146, 148, 160, 167, 168
Northern dynasties, 55
Nubia, 8, 11, 28, 29, 50, 51
Nunivagmiut people, 175
nuts, 190, 191

Odysseus, 89
Old Kingdom, 10
Old Stone Age, 9
olives, 107, 110
Olympic Games, 112–13
omens, 137
Opening the Mouth ceremony, 24
Opet Festival, 47
oracle bones, 56, 57, 66, 80
oracles, 93
oratory, 96–7
Osiris, 12, 16–17, 23, 24–5
Ostia, 130
ostraca, 38
ostracism, 97
Ottoman Turks, 169
oxen, 70

painting, 44–5, 51, 82, 132–3, 138, 146, 162
Pan, 99
paper, 31, 60, 80, 84
papyrus, 30, 31, 39, 44, 141
parfleches, 186, 198
Parthenon, 118
patol, 183
patricians, 135
Patwin people, 204
Pax Romana, 161
peasants, 14, 56, 68, 70–1, 74
Peloponnesian War, 120, 121
Pepy II, 10
perfume, 143
Pericles, 94, 115
Persia, 11, 50, 94, 122, 124
Persian Wars, 120–1
persimmons, 191
phalanx, 123
pharaohs, 9, 10–11, 12, 50, 51
Pheidias, 118
Philae Island, 28
Philip II of Macedon, 94, 122, 123
philosophy, 114
Phoenicians, 103
Pilate, Pontius, 162
pipes, 206–7
Piraeus, 94–5
play, 100, 101
playing cards, 182
plebeians, 135
poetry, 91, 103, 112
pollen ceremonies, 178, 186, 203
Poseidon, 98
pottery, 90, 91, 116–17, 148, 152, 160
powwows, 206, 207
Praetorian Guard, 158
priests/priestesses, 106, 114, 118, 132, 136, 137
Primavera, 142
printing, 80, 84
provinces, 146, 160, 168
Ptolemy dynasty, 124
Ptolemy I, 50
Ptolemy III, 50
Ptolemy XII, 50
Pueblo people, 194, 196

pyramids, 26–7
Pythian Games, 112, 113

Qebehsenuf, 22
Qin dynasty, 55, 58 –59
Qin Shi Huangdi, 58 –59, 81

Ramesses II, 8, 18, 20, 28, 29, 48
Ramesses III, 28, 47, 48
Raven, 172, 200
Ravenna, 130, 167, 169
Re, 12, 16–17, 23
red-figure ware, 117
Red Land, 8
red slipware, 160
reincarnation, 66
religion, 16–17, 50, 73, 93, 100, 109, 127, 132, 135, 136–7, 162–3, 167, 168, 169
Remus, 130
republic, 130, 134
reservations, 198, 214–15
retiarius, 154
Rhea Silvia, 130
rice, 54, 70
ring and pin, 183
rituals, 12, 18, 24, 178, 181, 200–9
roads, 144, 156–7
Roman orders, 119
Romans, 50, 51
Rome, 124, 126–7
Romulus, 130
Romulus Augustulus, 166
Rosetta Stone, 39
round houses, 196
rudders, 84

Sabines, 132
sacrifices, 56, 66, 98, 109, 112, 114
Sakhmet the Powerful, 16
salarium, 159
salmon, 192
Salmon and Cedar People, 174
Samnites, 132, 154
sanctuary, 18, 19
Saqqara, 8, 10
sarcophagus, 20, 164
sardonyx, 148
satyrs, 99
Sauk people, 175
scalps, 210, 211
Schliemann, Heinrich, 90, 91
scholar-gentry class, 60, 68, 74
science, 114–5
scribes, 38–9, 44
sculpture, 92, 93, 124
Sea Grizzly Bear, 200
seafaring, 88–9, 94–5
seasons, 30–1, 32
Second Intermediate Period, 37
seeds, 190, 191
Seleucus, 124
Seminole people, 179, 196
Senate/senators, 134, 135, 160
Seneca, 139
Seqenenre II, 41
servants, 34, 36, 37
Seth, 17, 23, 40
Sethos I, 19, 28
Seven Wonders of the World, 157
Severus, Septimius, 143, 160
shaduf, 33
shamans, 172, 208–9
Shang dynasty, 55, 56–7
sheep, 191, 217
Shen Nong, 70
shoes, 177, 187, 216
shops, 144–5, 150, 151
shrines, 136
sieges, 169
sign language, 175, 210
silk, 70, 74, 82
Silk Road, 54, 60, 62

silver, 63, 72, 74, 149, 152, 160, 180, 216, 217
Sioux people, 175, 182, 198, 204
Skywoman, 173
slaves, 13, 14, 36, 96, 100, 101, 104, 106, 107, 108, 109, 111, 112, 116, 135, 138, 139, 140, 143, 146, 147, 150, 151, 152, 154, 156, 162, 164
sleds, 186–7
Slow Bull, 209
snake rituals, 204, 208
snowshoes, 187
social order, 14–15, 135, 152
soldiers, 68, 70
Son of Heaven, 64
soothsayers, 157
Southern dynasties, 55
sowing, 32, 33
Spain, 146, 160, 168
Sparta, 94, 95, 102, 108, 120
Sphinx, 8, 11, 27
spirits, 200–1, 202, 205, 217
sport, 154–5, 182–3
Spring Festival, 76
stars, 26, 27
statues, 98, 104, 118–19, 124, 132, 144, 148
stickball, 182
Stone Age (Neolithic) period, 55
stone monuments, 26–7, 28, 45
Sui dynasty, 55
sweat lodges, 208
symposia, 110, 111

Tang dynasty, 55, 62–3, 64–5, 74, 75, 80, 83
Tarquin the Proud, 134
Taweret, 40
taxation, 14, 15, 32, 38, 58, 71, 160, 164, 165

tea, 62, 85
temples, 8, 11, 18–19, 26–9, 44, 51, 92, 93, 94, 95, 98, 114, 116, 118–19, 127, 136, 144
tepees, 196, 198–9
terracotta, 132
Terracotta Warriors, 59
tetrarchy, 165
theaters, 124, 144, 155
Thebes, 8, 51, 94
Theodora, Empress, 169
Theodosius I, 163, 166
Theodosius II, 169
Third Intermediate Period, 11
Thoth, 16, 24, 25
Thrace/Thracians, 154, 160
Three Kingdoms, 55
Thucydides, 121
Thunderbird, 200
Tiber, River, 130, 144
Tiberius, 152
tigers, 78
Titus, 150
Tivoli, 146
Tlingit people, 180, 194
tobacco, 174, 207
togas, 141, 142
tomahawks, 209
tomb goods, 58–59, 60–1, 62, 66, 73, 82
tombs, 20, 26–7, 44, 54, 66–7, 132, 162–3
tools, 20, 33, 39, 42, 45, 172, 192, 193
totems, 197, 200–1
toys, 35
trade, 12, 30, 62, 63, 88, 90, 92, 94–5, 110, 168, 194, 212, 213
Trail of Tears, 214
Trajan, 134, 150, 154, 160
transport, 30, 156

travel, 156–7
travois, 186
tribes, 174–5
triremes, 120
Trojan horse, 90–1
Trojan War, 90, 91, 121
Troy, 90–1
tule, 185, 186
tunics, 142
turquoise, 180, 216, 217
Tuscan order, 119
Tutankhamun, 23, 31
chariot, 48
gold funeral mask, 20
mummy, 21
tomb, 25
wooden throne, 13
Tuthmosis III, 44
tyrants, 96

ulu knife, 193
umbilical pouches, 178
Umbrians, 132
Ute people, 174

Valley of the Kings, 8
Vandals, 166, 167
vegetables, 146, 152, 190, 192
Vestal Virgins, 136–7
Via Appia, 157
villages, 174, 196–7
villas, 146–7
Virgil, 146
Visigoths, 166
vizier, 14
voting, 96, 97

walled cities, 90, 91, 94
wampum, 213

warfare, 48, 49, 56, 62, 94, 112, 120–1, 158–9, 160, 164, 173, 189, 210–11
warships, 120–1
water, 100, 108, 109
waterwheels, 147
weapons, 48, 90, 116, 123, 154–5, 158, 159, 173, 178, 210, 211
weaving and spinning, 100, 104, 105, 108, 176, 177, 217
weddings, 180–1
Wei River, 54
Western Empire, 164, 166–7
whales, 174, 192
wheat, 106, 110
wheelbarrows, 84, 85
wickiups, 196
wigwams, 196
wine making, 106–7
Wishram people, 180
women, 10, 12, 14, 15, 18, 30, 32, 100, 104, 105, 106, 108, 109, 110–1, 112, 114, 121
wool, 104, 105
work, 106–7, 116–17, 138, 140, 148–9
writing, 38–9, 58, 80–1, 92, 102–3, 140
Wu, Emperor, 68, 70
Wu Zetian, Empress, 64

Xia dynasty, 56
Xi'an, 55

Yang, Emperor, 61
Yangzi River, 54, 55, 61
Yellow River, 54, 55, 61, 71
Yin and Yang, 78
Yongtai, Princess, 66–7

Zeus, 98, 112, 122, 124, 127
Zhang Heng, 85
Zhou dynasties, 55

Picture Credits